# IF YOU'RE GOING
# TO LIVE IN THE COUNTRY

# IF YOU'RE GOING TO LIVE IN THE COUNTRY

THOMAS HAMILTON ORMSBEE,
RENEE RICHMOND HUNTLEY ORMSBEE

ISBN: 978-93-89701-53-1

Published:            -

LECTOR HOUSE LLP
E-MAIL: lectorpublishing@gmail.com

## A RIVERSIDE HOME RECONSTRUCTED FROM THE RUINS OF AN OLD MILL

*Photo by Samuel H. Gottscho. Robertson Ward, architect*

# IF YOU'RE GOING TO LIVE IN THE COUNTRY

BY

## THOMAS H. ORMSBEE
### AND
## RICHMOND HUNTLEY

DECORATIONS BY FRANK LIEBERMAN

**TO<br>CARROLL<br>AND<br>THERESE NICHOLS**

# ACKNOWLEDGMENTS

No book that covers so many phases of human relationships could be compiled without taking advice from those who are specialists. When we have wanted to know facts, we have freely turned to others whose detailed knowledge represented long experience. For this assistance we are particularly indebted to: M. Shaler Allen, Bruce Millar, Mrs. Herbert Q. Brown, and George S. Platts; also, to *House & Garden*, in which parts of this book appeared serially; and to Miss Eleanor V. Searing for many hours spent reading manuscript.

New Canaan, Conn.
April 1937

# CONTENTS

# LIST OF ILLUSTRATIONS

*Photo by John Runyn*

# INTRODUCTION

There is a beginning with everything. So far as this book is concerned, annual driving trips through Central Vermont are responsible. They were great events, planned months in advance. With a three-seated carriage and a stocky span good for thirty miles a day and only spirited if they met one of those new contraptions aglitter with polished brass gadgets, that fed on gasoline instead of honest cracked corn and oats, we took to the road. A newspaper man, vacation-free from Broadway first nights and operas sung by Melba, Sembrich, and the Brothers de Reszke, was showing his city-bred children his native hills and introducing them to the beauties of a world alien to asphalt pavements and brownstone fronts.

It was leisurely travel. When the road was unusually steep, to spare the horses, we walked. If Mother's eagle eye spotted a four-leaf clover, we stopped and picked it. If a bend in the road brought a pleasing prospect into view, the horses could be certain of ten minutes for cropping roadside grass. Most of all, no farmhouse nestling beneath wide-spread maples or elms went without careful consideration of Father's constant daydream, a home in the country.

These driving trips often included overnight stops with relatives living in villages undisturbed by the screech and thunder of freight and way trains, or with others living on picturesque old farms. Afterward there was always lively conversation concerning the possibilities of Cousin This or That's home as a country place. This reached fever heat after visits to Great Aunt Laura who lived in a roomy old house painted white with green blinds in a town bordering on Lake Champlain. A pair of horse-chestnut trees flanked the walk to the front door,—a portal unopened save for weddings, funerals, and the minister's yearly call.

From here could be seen the sweep of the main range of the Green Mountains. The kitchen doorway afforded a view of Mount Marcy and the Adirondacks never to be forgotten. It was the ancestral home with all the proper attributes, horse barn, woodshed, tool houses, and a large hay barn. Father's dream for forty years was to recapture it and settle down to the cultivation of rustic essays instead of its unyielding clay soil. However, he was first and last a newspaper man and his practical side told him that Shoreham was too far from Broadway. So it remained a dream.

His city-born and bred son inherited the insidious idea. Four years in a country college augmented it and, as time went on, the rumble of trucks and blare of neighboring radios turned a formerly quiet street on Brooklyn Heights into a bedlam and brought matters to a head. Great Aunt Laura's place was still too far away but explorers returning from ventures into the far reaches of Westchester County, and western Connecticut, had brought back tales of pleasantly isolated farmhouses with rolling acres well dotted with trees and stone fences. Here, thanks to the automobile and commuting trains, was the solution. A country place near enough to the city, so that the owner could have his cake and eat it, too.

After some months of searching and several wild goose chases, a modest little place was found. The original plan was to live there just a few weeks in the summer, possibly from June into September, but the period stretched a bit each year. Now it is the year around. We are but one of many families that have traded the noise and congestion of city life for the quiet and isolation of the open country. Nor do all such cling to the commuting fringe of the larger cities. A good proportion have their country homes some hours' distant, and the city is only visited at infrequent intervals.

Wherever his country place is located, however, there are certain problems confronting the city dweller who takes to rural life. They are the more baffling because they are not problems at all to his country-bred neighbors. The latter assume that any adult with a grain of common sense must know all about such trifles as rotten sills, damp cellars, hornets that nest in the attic, frozen pipes in winter, and wells that fail in dry seasons.

Of course, no one treatise can hope to serve as a guide for every problem that comes with life in the open country. This book is no compendium. It concerns itself only with the most obvious pitfalls that lie ahead of one inured to well-serviced city life.

# CHAPTER I

## WHY LIVE IN THE COUNTRY?

The urge to live in the country besets most of us sooner or later. Spring with grass vividly green, buds bursting and every pond a bedlam of the shrill, rhythmic whistle of frogs, is the most dangerous season. Some take a walk in the park. Others write for Strout's farm catalogues, read them hungrily and are well. But there are the incurables. Their fever is fed for months and years by the discomforts and amenities of city life. Eventually they escape and contentedly become box numbers along rural postal routes.

Why do city-bred people betake themselves to the country? The surface reasons are as many as why they are Republicans or Democrats, but the basic one is escape from congestion and confusion. For themselves or their children their goal is the open country beyond the suburban fringe. Here the children, like young colts, can be turned out to run and race, kick up their heels and enjoy life, free of warnings to be quiet lest they annoy the elderly couple in the apartment below or the nervous wreck the other side of that suburban privet hedge.

The day and night rattle and bang of the city may go unnoticed for years but eventually it takes its toll. Then comes a great longing to get away from it all. If family income is independent of salary earned by a city job, there is nothing to the problem. Free from a desk in some skyscraper that father must tend from nine to five, such a family can select its country home hours away from the city. Ideal! But few are so fortunate. Most of us consider ourselves lucky to have that city job. It is to be treated with respect and for us the answer lies in locating just beyond those indefinite boundaries that limit the urban zone. With the larger cities, this may be as much as fifty miles from the business center; with smaller ones the gap can be bridged speedily by automobile.

Going to live in the country, viewed dispassionately as an accountant's balance sheet, has attributes that can be recorded in black ink as well as those that require a robust crimson. If you really want a place where you need not be constantly rubbing elbows with the rest of the world; where you can cultivate something more ambitious than window boxes or an eight by ten pocket-handkerchief garden; where subways and street clatter can be forgotten; your black column will be far longer than the one in red. But if nothing feels so good to your foot as smooth unyielding pavements; if the multicolored electric sign of a moving picture palace is more entrancing than a vivid sunset; you are at heart a city bird, intended by temperament to nest behind walls of brick and steel. There is nothing you can do about it either. In the country the nights are so black; the birds at dawn too noisy; and Nature when she storms and scolds, is a fish-wife. Possibly you can learn to endure it all but will the game be worth the candle? Without true fondness for outdoors and an inner urge for a measure of seclusion, life in the country is drear. Don't attempt it.

But for those who care for the cool damp of evening dew; the first robin of spring hopping pertly across the grass; or a quiet winter evening with a good book or a radio program of their own choosing rather than that of the people living across the hall; country life is worth every cent of its costs and these bear lightly.

Along Fifth avenue, New York, not far from the Metropolitan Museum, is a typical town house. A man of means maintains it for social and business reasons. But he does not live there. His intimates know that only a few minutes after the last dinner guest has departed, his chauffeur will drive him some twenty miles to a much simpler abode on a secluded dirt road. Here, he really lives. Whistling tree toads replace the constant whir of buses and taxicabs.

Most of us cannot be so extravagant. We are fortunate to have one home, either in the city or the country. Renting or buying it entails sacrifices, and maintaining it has its unexpected expenses that always come at the wrong time. What do those who live beyond the limits of cities and sophisticated villages gain by hanging their crane with the rabbits and woodchucks?

First, country living is the answer to congestion. Even the most modest country cottage is more spacious than the average city apartment. Life in such a house may be simple but not cramped. There is light and air on all sides. This may seem unimportant but did you ever occupy an apartment where the windows opened on a court or were but a few feet from the brick wall of another warren for humans? If the sun reached your windows an hour or two a day, you were lucky. In a country house there is sunlight somewhere on pleasant days from morning to night. That difference can only be understood by those who have known both ways of living.

In town, light and air cost money; along the rural postal routes it is as much a part of the scheme of things as summer insects or winter snows. And it may have a very definite bearing on the well being of all members of the family. Some suffer more than they realize from lack of sunlight. Frequently it is the children and, with many families, decision to move countryward is on their account. In fact, there be some, where father and mother, if they consulted their own preferences, would stay in a city apartment convenient to theatres and shops, with friends and acquaintances close at hand. But their small children lack robustness. The parents try everything, careful diet, adequate hours of sleep and all the other recommendations of scientific child rearing. Still the little arms and legs continue to be spindling. Tonics and cod liver oil fail to get rid of that pinched look, the concomitant of too little sunlight and too many hours indoors. In desperation such a family betakes itself to the country. The children weather tan. They respond to the more placid life and gradually gain the much sought after hardiness. Nature has been the physician without monthly bills for house or office treatments.

The children are not the only ones who gain. Healthy adults renew their energy and crave activity. Here opportunity lies close at hand. It may be swinging a golf club or going fishing. It may be such unorganized methods of stretching muscles and increasing breathing as pushing a lawn mower, raking leaves or weeding the delphinium border. All these sports and homely out-of-door duties and pleasures are nearby, many of them just the other side of the front door. Those classed as sports may require a country club membership but even this is on a more modest scale.

In fact, all potent are the economies made possible by leaving city or closely built suburb. House and land, either bought or rented, comes cheaper and is more ample. Along with this basic saving there are a number of others that help to leave something from the family income at the end of the year. Clothes last longer in the country and wardrobe requirements are simpler. Similarly, there is a distinct decrease in the money spent for amusements. When the nearest moving picture house is five miles away it is easy to stay at home. Going to the movies is not a matter of just running around the corner and so done automatically once or twice a week. Then there are such things as doctor's bills. While sickness, like taxes, visits every family no matter where it lives, we have found that we actually have less need of medical care living in the sticks than we did in town. Also the charges for competent care by both doctors and dentists are lower.

For the family inclined to delve in the soil, a definite saving can be accomplished by tending a vegetable garden, raising small fruits and berries, and even maintaining a hen roost. Some people (I would I could honestly include myself) have a gift for making things grow and getting crops that are worth the work that has gone into them. Likewise there is such a thing as possessing a knack with that unresponsive and perverse creature, the hen. Possibly good gardening and an egg-producing hen-yard are the result of willingness to take infinite pains but, out of my disappointments and half successes, I am more inclined to hold that it is luck and predestination. So, I have reduced agricultural activities sharply, but I do know families where each fall finds cellar shelves groaning under cans of fruits and vegetables, products of the garden, and foretelling distinct economies in purchases of canned goods or fresh vegetables.

One of the largest single savings that country life makes possible is elimination of private school tuition. Theoretically city public schools are good enough for anybody's children. Actually most good neighborhoods have an undesirable slum just around the corner and the public school is for the children of both. So, many city-dwelling families, not from snobbishness but because they do not want their young hopefuls to acquire slum manners and traits, dig deep into their bank accounts and send their children to private schools.

Seldom is this necessary in the country, especially if the educational system is investigated beforehand. Instead, the children start in a good consolidated graded school, proceed through the local high school, and are prepared for college with all the cost of tuition included in the tax bill that must be paid anyway. The children are none the worse for this less guarded education. They are, in fact, benefited for they have a democratic background that makes later life easier.

Besides these creature comforts and financial gains, there are the intangibles. Chief of these is that indescribable something, country peace. All the family responds to it. It is impossible to maintain the highly-keyed, nervous tension that characterizes city life when the domestic scene is surrounded by open fields or an occasional bit of woodland. The placid calm soothes frayed nerves and works wonders in restoring balance and perspective toward family and business problems. The harassed come to realize the inner truth of "God's in his heaven, all's right with the world."

Along with this, the family transplanted from the city gradually comes to know the genuine joys of much simpler pleasures. Separated from the professional recreations that beckon so engagingly in cities and the larger towns, adults and children alike develop resources within themselves. They learn that they can be just as contented with homely enjoyments as they ever were when they sat passively and were amused by some one who made it his profession. A tramp through the woods in the fall when there is a tang of frost in the air; the satisfaction of a long-planned flower bed in full bloom; a winter evening with a log fire blazing on the living-room hearth; are simple but as genuine as any of the pleasures known to city folk. Better yet, they are not exhausting. "Few people are strong enough to enjoy their pleasures," a friend once wisely observed. In the main, however, those of the country are less taxing and leave one refreshed which, after all, is the true purpose of recreation.

Against these gains of country living the costs must also be reckoned. These, as stated earlier, will hardly be felt if the individual really likes the country in its smiling moods as well as its frowning ones. One which the family recently separated from city ways may find hardest to accept is a demand for self-reliance. If the furnace will not burn, a water pipe springs a leak, a mid-winter blizzard deposits a snowdrift that all but blocks the front door, father or some one else must rise to the situation.

The country home has no janitor. The nearest plumber is two or five miles away. No gang of snow shovelers knocks at the door with offers to attack the mislocated snow at a price, albeit the highest they think the traffic will bear. Pioneer-like, some or all of the family must turn to and cope with such situations. Doing so, whether temporary like closing a pipe valve to stop the cascading water until the plumber arrives, or permanent like mastering the idiosyncrasies of the furnace, has its reward. From oldest to youngest, after a year or so there comes a sense of ability to cope with the unforeseen rather than to stand meekly by waiting for George to do it.

**THE OGDEN HOUSE, FAIRFIELD, CONN. BUILT BEFORE 1705, IT HAS BEEN RESTORED TO PRESERVE THE ORIGINAL DETAILS**

*Miss Mary Allis*

Again, it is not always smiling June with gentle breezes. There are also January, February and March, the months winter really settles to his task and delivers, as he will, snow storms, or spells of abnormally cold weather that make the house hard to heat and may freeze pipes. There are also rainy spells of two or three days' duration that come any time, spring, summer or fall. It is fun to be in the country when the sun shines. There are so many things to do and see out-of-doors. It is totally different when it rains and rains and still keeps on until everything outside is dripping and sodden. Then comes the testing time. Child or grown-up must accept such bad weather and make light of its restrictions, or country living is hard indeed. But did you ever put on boots and oilskins and go for a long walk in the rain just for the pure joy of it? Try it some time. You will see fields and bushes with different eyes and hear that most musical of all country sounds, the rush of tiny brooks in full flood. Even the birds have their rainy day manners and ways.

The most ardent country advocate, however, cannot deny that in some respects such a life has certain expenses not entered in the budget of families living in town. First and foremost, if father has his city job there is the monthly commutation book as well as the occasional railroad fares when other members of the family go to the city. There is no argument about it. These are added expenses but they are more than offset by reductions in the fixed charges. Also by selecting where you will live, transportation costs can be controlled.

Expenditures incident to entertaining are another matter. One of the pleasantest things about living out-of-town is the week-end. From Friday night or Saturday noon until Monday morning the city is forgotten. Of course, part of the time, you will want to share these days with friends still cooped in apartments. Week-end guests vary the picture and are worth both the effort and money entertaining them involves. But don't think that will be all. No country-living family is safe from either friends or casual acquaintances in these days of motor cars. They will appear most unexpectedly and assume that you are as delighted to see them as they are to have you as an objective for a Sunday afternoon motor trip.

At first it is flattering to have people come so far just to see you. Then the novelty of it wears a little thin and you begin to realize that frequently Monday morning finds the refrigerator swept bare. In time it will dawn on you that part of the up-keep of a country home revolves around feeding your self-invited guests. It would not be so bad if they would telephone ahead so that you could be prepared, but that is not one of the rules of the game. Instead, it is taken for granted that living in the country, you have a never-failing pantry. The solution lies in preparedness. From early spring until about Thanksgiving time, have in reserve some simple supplies for an acceptable afternoon tea or Sunday night supper.

One household of my acquaintance always has large pitchers of milk, a supply of crackers, two or three kinds of cheese, a platter of sandwiches, home-made cake and a hot drink. As many as wish are welcome to come at the last moment for this standard Sunday night supper. Its simplicity has earned this repast a wide reputation and it is considered a great lark to go there. Incidentally, this truly rural supper is so inexpensive that it matters little how many are on hand Sunday evenings. Also the chore of washing dishes after the last guests have gone is reduced to lowest terms, likewise an item not to be overlooked.

This trend toward country living, now so far flung as to be a characteristic of American life, is not just a fad. It has been a slow steady growth and has behind it a tradition of a century and more. When our larger commercial centers first began to change from villages to compact urban communities, there were those who found even these miniature cities far too congested. It was incomprehensible to them that a family should exist without land enough for such prime requisites as a cow, a hen-yard, and a vegetable garden. No family that really lived and properly enjoyed the pleasures of the table could be without them. Besides, epidemics of yellow fever came with summer as naturally as sleighing with winter.

So for health and good living they began to move far into the country, — that is, three or four miles out of town, — and stage coach routes were established to transport the heads of such families to and from business either the year around or for the summer months. These stages or the private carriages of the more ostentatious were, of course, horse-drawn which limited the distance which could be traveled.

The next step was the railroads. Hardly were they practical means of transportation that could be relied on day in and day out, before commutation tickets were offered for those hardy enough to endure daily trips of a dozen miles or more between home and office. Gradually the peaceful farming villages surrounding cities were transformed into something new to the American scene, the suburban town, but it remained impractical for most people to live farther from the station than a convenient walk. When electric car lines were added, the distance was extended materially and the farm lands just outside these suburban towns took on new value. Near car lines, they could be sold to those not primarily concerned with agriculture. The interurban electric roads also made many so-called abandoned farms in various parts of the country practical for families who wished to live farther from commercial centers either throughout the year or for the summer months, since they provided that great essential, a quick means of getting to shopping towns. Still great sections of back country, too far from railroads and electric car lines, remained strictly rural.

Finally the automobile, made inexpensive enough for families of average income and provided with that great innovation, the self-starter, changed it all. This was not so very long ago. Approximately with the World War came the moderate-priced car that need not be cranked by hand. Driving it was no longer a sporting male occupation too often marred by broken arms and sprained wrists, the painful outcome of hand-cranking when the motor "back-fired." With the self-starter car driving went feminine. Mother, as well as father, could and did drive. It was now practical for automobile owning families to live farther from railroad stations and villages.

Unnoticed at the time, a new sort of pioneering began. City-dwelling people turned hungry eyes toward the cheap country farmhouses located beyond limits of horse and carriage travel. By 1920, this trend was in full swing and greatly expedited by the program of highway improvement and rebuilding that spread across the country.

With a quick and easy means of travel, good roads, telephone and electric service, farmhouses which but a few years before had been as isolated as when Horace Greeley was thundering, "Go West, young man, go West," were isolated no more. Prices rose but not beyond the purchasing power of those who sought escape from city congestion or the restrictions of fifty-foot suburban lots. The gasoline age had done it. It had married rural peace to rapid transportation. If you had to earn your living in the city, it was no longer required that you and your family live in its midst. A tranquil country home was yours if you would reach for it.

# CHAPTER II

## SELECTING THE LOCATION

It is to be questioned whether any city dwelling family suddenly determines to move to the country. Such changes in one's way of life are not decided as casually as trading in the old car for a model of the current year. Usually the decision to pioneer backward is reached so gradually that those who take the step can hardly tell in retrospect just when the die was cast. A vacation or summer in the country may have put it in mind. Then a period of vague indecision follows when city and country appear about equally attractive. Suddenly some chance happening turns the scale.

A week-end invitation for cider making in the Hoosatonic Valley in early November would seem harmless enough, but from it dated our own determination to cease to be city dwellers. It must be admitted that the stage-setting was perfect. A twenty-mile ride on the evening of our arrival through the sharp clear air with a full harvest moon hanging high in the heavens, while along the way lights twinkled hospitably from the farmhouses that dotted the countryside. A bright crisp morning and a breakfast of sausages, griddle cakes and syrup. This would have been viewed with lack-luster eye in our overheated city apartment but was somehow just right in this fireplace heated country room with a tang of chill in the far corners.

Later we were to find that plenty of November nights could be raw and stormy; that fireplaces could sulk and give out such grudging heat as to make the room wholly chill. But none of this appeared on that memorable week-end. It waxed warm enough at midday for all of the outdoor pleasures that the country affords. We were in congenial company and evening found us with a sense of peace and well-being that more than balanced the loss of a theatre or dinner party in town. We were guilty of the usual platitudes about "God's country and the normal way to live" and knew they were that but didn't care.

However, there was no rushing around to get a place right across the way. A whole winter went by, pleasantly spent doing the usual things. Then came spring, a season that not even the city can wholly neutralize. There were a number of seemingly aimless Sunday trips beyond the urban fringe. There was considerable casual comment on various houses in attractive settings. One charming old place ideally located on a back road proved to be part of a water-shed reservation. Another equally charming plaster house was "too far out." As we admitted that, we realized that we had joined that not inconsiderable group who "want to have their cake and eat it too." That is, we really wanted a place in the country but we wanted it near enough so that the desk of the very necessary and important job could be reached without too much effort. Also the idea of an occasional evening in town was not to be dismissed lightly.

Such humdrum items as railroad time tables were consulted. Having decided that the ideal location would be one in which the time required for train trip and motoring from house to station would come within an hour, we limited our search to that section just beyond the suburban fringe in Connecticut and Westchester County, New York. We had no clear idea of the type of house we wanted, save that it be old and of good lines. We looked with and without the aid of real estate dealers. We deluged our friends already living in the country with queries.

We found a disheartening number of fine old houses, located just wrong. There was a splendid, two-story brick house with hall running through the middle. But it stood in the commercial section of a village, its door steps flush with the sidewalk, and was hemmed in on one side by a gas station. There was a neat little story-and-a-half stone house with picket fence, old-fashioned rose bushes, and beautiful shade trees. It had once been the parsonage of the neighboring church. Unhappily the old churchyard lay between.

Now, we are not people who whistle determinedly when passing a marble orchard at midnight nor do we see white luminous shapes flitting among the tombstones. But daily gazing upon one's final resting place, we felt might, in time, prove depressing. Besides, we were by no means certain that our friends had developed the callous indifference of a young couple we heard of years later. Curiously free of inhibitions, these two people bought an attractive old farmhouse with a family burying lot located a fair distance from the house. The little plot with its eight or ten simple headstones was unobtrusive and rather gave an air of family roots deep in the soil, a quality all too rare in America. These young vandals could not let well enough alone. They uprooted the headstones and laid them end to end for a walk to their front door! They were considering the plot itself as a possible tennis court when outraged public opinion forced them to put the stones back. In fact, the general hostility was so marked that they finally abandoned the place and it was later sold at a distinct loss.

But back to the little gray parsonage; its location and the fact that train service in its vicinity was poor, were the two deciding votes against it. Another attractive house in a good location was ruled out because our car got stuck in a spring hole practically in sight of it. A mile or so of dirt road to the station is no drawback, provided it is passable at all times of the year. This one was obviously poor, even in summer. Finally a real estate broker showed us a picture of a modest 18th century farm cottage. We visited the place one dreary sunless day in late March, investigated the neighborhood, determined the time required to drive to the nearest railroad station, and bought it, all in one week.

In general, we are not sure that such haste is advisable. There were certain disadvantages that we did not observe; there were others where we turned a blind eye because we were infatuated with the place and determined to have it. Fortunately time has taken care of practically all of these. In short, we have come to believe that a place in the country is, like marriage, just what you make it. In both cases, though, one's emotions should be under control, so here are a few salient points for the searcher after a suitable location.

First and foremost, decide on the sort of life you wish to lead. Then pick your location to fit it. If you are not chained to a city desk five days a week but at best make only one or two weekly trips there, a railroad journey of two or three hours is endurable especially when a highly attractive place lies at the end. For such a person, the radius in which to look for likely places is much extended and the farther out, the more advantageous the prices. But for one individual so fortunately situated, there are more than a hundred who must choose a place near enough for daily trips to the city.

For the latter the ideal situation is, as stated before, an hour from house to office. That is the ideal but, in all honesty, we must admit that few attain it. The average country commuter is a born optimist on this point and will unblushingly distort facts in a manner to put the most ardent fisherman to shame. But figures don't lie. If the time table, say between Stamford, Connecticut, and the Grand Central, New York, gives its fastest running time as fifty minutes, it means exactly that. You may plan to hurtle through the air at sixty miles an hour to the station but traffic and road conditions will not always let you. Besides, what is the hurry? Allow twenty or thirty minutes instead of fifteen for a normal run of twelve miles and have peace of mind. That gives you an hour and ten or fifteen minutes between your house and the city. Add the time needed to get from the train to your office and you know what is before you. We mention this station trip of twelve miles as about the maximum for the hardy commuter although there are a few who take more punishment than that. Of course if the perfect place can be found only four to six miles from the station that is all the better.

Transportation is an all important consideration both as regards time and expense. There are beautiful countrysides fairly near large centers that are so hampered by poor train service as to be almost out of the question for the everyday commuter. Of course, there may be an adequate service or it may be practical to drive to and from business. The latter is not at all uncommon with the country areas near the smaller industrial centers. Here the fortunate commuter is free from exacting train schedules; a five or ten minutes' drive sees him outside the city limits, and another twenty or thirty may find him rolling into his own driveway. Smooth sailing between office and home depend only on a reliable car and good roads.

One should make sure the latter are passable in the winter at all times. For instance, are the Town Fathers liberal with the snow plow? Can its cheery hum be heard even at midnight if a heavy fall of snow makes it necessary? Does it come down the little dirt road where your modest acres are located? These are questions all commuters should ask whether their journey cityward is made entirely by automobile or partly by train. Further, whatever means of transportation are used, the monthly cost should be reckoned carefully. It is one of the largest single items involved in this scheme of living in the country and working in the city.

There is also the question of food and other household supplies. Granted one no longer expects to run around the corner for a loaf of bread or a dozen eggs that may have been left off the morning shopping lists, just how far away is the nearest grocer? Is he at all receptive to the idea of making an occasional delivery in the outlying districts? How about the rubbish collector, if any; the milkman; the purveyors of ice, coal and wood? Are there a lighting system in the vicinity, telephone facilities, and so forth? These last need not be deciding factors, all other things being equal. They are simply matters to investigate. It is then for the family to decide whether to do without any or all of them if necessary.

Besides in a wisely chosen location, these, though lacking at first, are soon added as the demand grows. When we began our own experiment in country living, it was with difficulty that we got even a telephone installed. Instead of electricity, our evenings were lighted by candles or kerosene lamps and our meals were cooked on an oil stove. Grocers and other tradesmen didn't even know how to get to the little area. Yet within three years enough other people like us had moved into the vicinity to warrant extension of electric service through the neighborhood, and a milk route, rubbish service, deliveries of laundry, food, ice, and other household needs were soon added. The Fuller brush man has for years known the way to our door and now even our Sunday newspapers are delivered, although we are six miles from the nearest news stand.

This brings us to the question of neighborhood, which is important. Beware of a place too near a small factory settlement. The latter is apt to grow and destroy the peace you have come so far to get. Besides, your property value will decline in direct ratio. We once knew a charming place set high on a hill with neat hedges, shrubs, and arbors reminiscent of England, birthplace of the man who built and developed it. The family that bought the property forgot to look down at the foot of the hill. If they had, they would have seen a large and efficient looking factory and could have read the signs accordingly.

The disadvantages of a country home located close to a hamlet inhabited by old native stock families that have degenerated should be weighed carefully. Such people resent what they consider unwarranted intrusion by newcomers and have many underhanded ways of expressing their antagonism. Of course, if these settlers are merely tenants and the region shows distinct signs that a number of city pioneers are about to buy property there, it may be a gamble worth taking, since one can always buy property cheaper before a boom than after it has set in. Also, these settlements are frequently located in the most beautiful sections of the country. Some of the houses are quaint farm cottages that only need a thorough cleaning and a little intelligent restoration to make them attractive homes for any one.

Again, some of the most picturesque and desirable locations are off on byroads. They are much to be preferred to property directly on the main highway since they are well away from the roar of traffic; and if there are children or pets, one need not be constantly on the alert to keep them from straying off the premises. However, half a mile off the main highway answers the purpose as well as a longer distance and one must be sure that half mile is passable at all times of the year.

We have in mind one young couple who bought a place in Vermont. It stands well up on a hill and the view is worth going many miles to see. A picturesque dirt road winds a crooked mile up to it. Very attractive for summer but these two live there the year around. The snow drifts deep in winter, and early spring and late fall find the mud so deep that the average car bogs down hopelessly. Thus, they are virtual prisoners during these seasons. Of course that is an extreme case and even here the road can be made passable but only at heavy expense which must be borne principally by the householder.

Lastly, in selecting the locality for your experiment in country living, if there are children consideration of schools is essential. The ratings and relative standings of graded and high schools in various localities, may be easily obtained through state educational authorities, college entrance boards, and similar organizations. But even where the rating report is good, personal investigation is advisable. Certain social elements enter in, despite the sound and democratic principles underlying the American public school system.

For example, a would-be country dweller leased a house, with option to buy, in a very good neighborhood. House, location, and surroundings exactly pleased and it was a scant ten minutes from the station on a good road. The school system was well rated but the graded school for this section drew a majority of its pupils from a textile mill settlement two or three miles away. The children of the English spinners and weavers were decent, well-behaved youngsters but their speech was distinctly along cockney lines. Within a few months the three small sons of the new country dweller had developed habits of speech native to the English textile towns. Stern correction at home availed little and their parents abandoned the idea of buying in that locality. Instead, another was selected after personal inspection of the school to which the three boys would go. The new home is not, in some respects, as attractive as the other nor is it as convenient for commuting, but one cannot have everything. They are content and the small boys are once more expressing themselves with a New England accent.

In inspecting both the graded and high schools of a neighborhood that pleases you, the obvious things are the buildings, school bus service, play space, provisions for school lunches and so forth. These are tangible and can be readily observed. Much more important are the intangibles. These include the scholastic standing of the particular school; the pedagogical ability and personality of the individual teachers; and, finally, whether those who manage village, borough, or town governments, provide adequate school appropriations.

Schools that really educate children can be operated on starvation budgets but, more often than not, the quality of teaching suffers. Likewise the schools of a town reflect the capacity and ability of those in charge. To judge this, make it a point to meet the local school superintendent. If there is a parent-teachers association, a frank discussion with its leader is an excellent idea. From talks like these you can sometimes gather cogent information that neither superintendent nor member of the school association would or could put in writing. If possible observe the school while it is in session. The attitude of teachers and children should enable you to form an estimate of it as a whole.

In determining the scholastic standing of a high school, its rating by college entrance boards, the success in college of recent graduates, and kindred data can be readily obtained and will tell a complete story. However, under present conditions, there are some excellent high schools which pay little or no attention to college preparation because relatively few pupils intend to enter college. If this condition prevails at the high school your children would normally attend and your plans for them include college or technical school, recognition of it is important. A year or two in a good private school that makes a specialty of college preparation is probably the answer. But don't wait until a son or daughter is nearly through the local high school to discover this lack of specific preparation.

If, on the other hand, you do not intend to send your children to the schools where tuition is included in the tax bill, be just as careful in judging the private school. The term private means just what it says, it is open to children whose parents make private or separate payment for their education. This condition, however, is no guarantee that the quality of teaching will excel or even equal that of the free or public institution.

The private ventures are not under as rigid supervision as those supported by tax revenues and we have known of instances where the former were distinctly below standard. With a private day school having relatively few pupils and a tuition revenue only slightly above the cost of operation, it requires considerable strength of character for its owner not to gloss over a pupil's shortcomings. If dealt with impartially, these might mean that darling Willie would be withdrawn and sent elsewhere. Loss of tuition is the nightmare of the head of such a school. Hence, fear of financial loss, dread of disagreeable interviews with parents, or misguided leniency can have a very bad effect on the education and training of the pupils.

Yet there are small day schools and larger institutions with both day and resident pupils that give superior training. It is largely a matter of the attitude and capacity of the principal or head. If he or she is a real teacher and has good assistants, the children will be well taught, regardless of the physical plant. So, in choosing a private school, make sure the education it affords is worth the tuition father pays.

Putting the children in a private school necessitates one thing more. That is transportation. Sometimes a private bus takes care of this matter. If not, mother must be tied to a daily schedule of driving the youngsters to and from school. This usually entails a second car. Here, as with other matters, the initial cost is by no means all; there is the up-keep. This should not be overlooked, for in the twelve years between the first grade and the last high school year, it becomes an increasing burden as school hours lengthen and athletic activities become, to the children at least, supremely important.

# CHAPTER III

## SHOPPING FOR PROPERTY

The early American pioneer pushed into the wilderness looking for a likely spot to settle. When he had either found it or had traveled as far as he could, he staked out land and built a rude shelter for his family until such time as he could afford better. Today's pioneer decides whether he will have a house and five or more acres in commuting distance of the city, a farm several hours away from it, or a sporting estate. Then, still seated in an easy chair, he reaches for real estate advertising as found in newspaper, magazine or folder.

For the first, nothing is better than newspaper classified advertising, particularly that found in the Sunday paper. If he would have a farm far from the madding crowd, there are the farm catalogues issued by a variety of real estate organizations. These can be most helpful if intelligently read. And the prospective buyer of a fancy farm or sporting estate will do best to turn to the advertising columns of those magazines where the editorial scope deals with that type of country life.

Consulting such advertising for whatever kind of country home is wanted will give the prospective buyer some definite impressions. Of course he won't know what any of the places actually look like, though reading between the lines may give him some idea; but he will at least have gleaned a little information as to prices in a given locality and have the names of brokers with offerings that might be of interest. A decade ago, if one really wanted a country place one began looking at actual pieces of property at this point, either with or without a broker. During the past two or three years, however, a novel source of information regarding such property has come into being.

**AN OLD FARMHOUSE IN THE ROUGH**

*Photo by John Runyon*

It is somewhat of a cross between a news reel moving picture theatre and a real estate broker's office. There is a projection room, a small moving picture machine, and an extensive file of films of various properties that are on the market. Here the prospective buyer is shown shorts of all those listed with that particular clearing house. After the showing, if one or more places appeal sufficiently so that the prospect wants to visit them, he is given the broker's name and address. This saves much time and hours of travel for all concerned.

In an hour or two spent so shopping, you can get first impressions of more places than you could possibly visit in a month of week-ends. Thus you can limit your selection of places to be visited. The cost of this novel method of showing property is met by an arrangement whereby seller and broker reward the picture house if the sale is consummated.

When you actually begin to look at property, a few don'ts are in order if you would steer a fair course to the country home you have in mind.

Don't expect any place to have all the requirements included in your mental picture.

Don't buy a place that does not appeal to you. Each year you will like it less.

Don't buy a bargain without finding out why it is below the prevailing price. Only too often it proves extremely expensive.

Don't disparage a piece of property with the naive idea that by so doing the price will be lowered. You only arouse resentment on the part of the owner.

Don't make a pest of yourself by too frequent visits to a place that attracts you.

Don't try to eliminate the real estate broker. If he really knows his territory, his services are worth far more than his fee which is paid by the seller anyway.

Don't lose your temper during the negotiations that must precede the terms of sale. You may lose the place that just suits you.

Don't expect to buy property with wooden money. That custom went out shortly after 1929.

If you can subscribe to these points, you are one of those who really want a country home and will eventually find one. Those who only think they do will stumble over some detail and then settle back with a plaintive, "We would love to move to the country if we could only find a place like yours." Castles in the air have everything, for imagination builds them; but those planted four square upon the earth always have certain "outs," even though you buy a perfect building site and put the house you have dreamed of thereon.

Personally, we have always wanted a little gray house mellowed by the summers and winters of at least a century. What we bought was a small story-and-a-half farm cottage with outer walls of weathered shingles, painted red. It is old. During the Revolution, a British soldier was slain in the very doorway as he came out with loot from the upper rooms. It would undoubtedly be a haunted house in England but here our eyes are holden and we have never seen him, nor have any of our guests.

We still admire gray stone houses of which there are plenty down in the Pennsylvania Dutch country but we are honestly suited with what we have. Its general outline is akin to the house we envisioned and the mellow tone of its red-shingled exterior has a charm of its own. True, the grounds are lacking in those little irregularities that enable one to develop secluded spots and charming rock gardens. No brook runs through them and there is no high point of land where one looks off to a brilliant summer sunset or hills blue with haze. It is just a pleasing peaceful spot and we like it.

In short, have all the preconceived notions you want but keep an open mind as well as an open eye. We know of two or three families that are absolutely satisfied with their country homes, yet are perfectly frank in admitting that they are in no way the type of house or setting indicated by their preliminary specifications. They saw them in the course of their search and, despite the divergence, recognized that they met their demands.

One of our friends had steadfastly insisted that his country house must sit on a hilltop where he could have a view, see the sun rise and set, and be cooled by a fine breeze on the most torrid day. He bought an entire farm just to get an upland pasture with the required hilltop. Luckily he called in an architect and was mercifully prevented from getting what he wanted. His house was finally built on a sightly but sheltered spot about halfway below the high point of his land. He has since learned that during the winter months the prevailing westerly winds so sweep that hilltop that heating a house placed there would be expensive and difficult. Also, these same winds would be apt to work havoc with his shrubbery and flower garden.

On the contrary, don't let yourself be stampeded into buying something that definitely does not appeal, just because you are a little tired of looking but are bound to live in the country anyway. Real estate dealers and would-be helpful friends may have rallied around and, after showing you a score or more parcels of land, begin hinting that you are hard to please. Possibly, but just remember that your money purchases the place and that you, not they, will have to live there. Two people once spent years looking for a place within easy commuting distance of Philadelphia. Friends and brokers became exhausted and fell by the way. Word was passed around among the latter that these people were "just lookers and there was no use bothering with them." One day a broker, hoping to be rid of them, showed a piece of property so unsightly and generally run down that he thought no one could possibly want it. To his amazement, they liked it, saw its possibilities and, after proper investigation, bought for cash with never a quibble over the price. They showed rare intelligence in restoring both house and grounds and are living contentedly there today.

Most of us, though, who really want a country home are of no mind to spend years looking for one. It may be that the lease on the city apartment is due to expire in a few months and one must decide whether it is to be renewed or not. There may be children in the family who are in urgent need of the fresh air and outdoor life of the country. Under such circumstances, it is often a real advantage to rent a place for a year with option to buy. One learns both the good and bad qualities of a house in that time at probably no greater cost than continued rental for a city establishment. Further, if you decide to buy it at the end of the year, the rental paid may apply on the purchase price.

You can thus have plenty of time to look over other property in the vicinity. Perhaps it may be impossible to find a house that really pleases, but you do discover an ideal site. It may be a fine old orchard. It may be a tree-shaded spot with an old cellar marking the place where a house once stood. It may be an undeveloped hillside. In such an event, you have the advantage of either building a house to your liking, or finding an old one and moving it there.

Be very sceptical about "bargains" in your search. Relatively few people underestimate the value of their possessions. Perhaps they are really willing to sell at a sacrifice "because father can't stand the cold winters any more" or "because we like to feel the place is in good hands." But it would seem more reasonable that father's declining years in Florida or California would be sweetened in direct ratio to the amount realized on his property. So look well for the real reason. The house may be unduly expensive to maintain. It may be so badly built that bigger and better repairs become a constant drain on the family purse. There may be something so wrong with the adjoining property that one must either buy that, too, or give up any idea of living on the spot with any comfort or pleasure.

Back in 1928, a man bought a comparatively new house and eight acres of land for a sum far below the prevailing prices in the vicinity. The grounds were attractive and the lawn well shaded with fine old maples. He acquired this "bargain" in the late fall without benefit of real estate dealer. In fact, he boasted of his acumen to a broker who had originally shown him several other pieces of property in the section.

"I told you there were cheaper places," he chortled, "and the owner gave me the advantage of the broker's commission, too. Come out next spring and see what a bargain I found." In late May there came a wail for help from the cocksure buyer. A few days of unseasonably warm weather and a strong east wind had revealed the reason for the bargain. Back of a wooded area to the rear of his holding, was a combination hog farm and refuse dump. The owner of it got little or no rental from the tenant farmer who carried on his noisome business but he was well aware of its nuisance value to his new neighbor. Here indeed was a situation requiring the services of that middle man, the real estate broker. The latter was a good business man and by using all his guile, he eventually acquired the hog farm for his client at a fair price. But even at that, the man now had ten additional acres that he didn't want and couldn't use. When the cost of the added land and clearing it of refuse had been met, his place was not the bargain it had seemed originally.

This does not mean that there are never any country places to be had at real bargains. It is a case of being keen enough or lucky enough to locate one. There can be a number of legitimate reasons why a piece of property is on the market at a price below its general worth. There may be urgent financial reasons why the owner must sell. In this unhappy situation he cannot be too firm as to price and will usually accept a sum actually below the market value in order to salvage a fair proportion of what he may have invested.

Another type of bargain is that of property that has only recently become available for country homes through the construction of a new motor highway or some other major development. For example, the electrification of the Pennsylvania Railroad and a concrete automobile road from Trenton, New Jersey, into Bucks County, Pennsylvania, have brought old farms in and around Doylestown,

Pennsylvania, within an hour and a half of New York City. This condition has not existed long and Bucks County farms on an acreage basis may still be bought distinctly cheaper than in practically any other section equi-distant in travel time from New York.

Again, some particular place may be owned by an estate with a number of heirs who want their money. None of them feels inclined to take over the property and pay off the others. All are in a hurry to get their share of what Uncle Henry left. Eventually the property goes at a partition sale which is the bargain basement of real estate. Partition sales and heirs hungry for ready money are keenly watched by those who buy purely for investment and with the expectation of resale to some one wanting a country home. Hence the ultimate consumer rarely benefits. But occasionally the regular investor finds the matter of resale neither as simple nor as rapid as he had expected.

For some years we watched a charming little place that a real estate investor had acquired at such a partition sale. It was first offered "in the rough." Then the abandoned household gear and accumulated trash were removed. With growing nervousness the investor applied a coat of paint to the house and hung neat painted shutters at the windows. He tore down dilapidated outbuildings and converted the barn into a garage. The place still hung unplucked on his commercial tree. After three dismal years he parted with it at a price but little above that paid at the partition sale.

It was a desirable property but the investor had been over greedy and had put his original asking price far too high. By the time he was chastened enough to listen to reasonable offers, most of the prospective buyers had crossed that place off their list. The ultimate purchaser acquired a real bargain by happening along at the psychological moment when the investor was sick of his deal and ready to part with it at little or no profit.

This was, of course, very much a matter of luck. It is also a matter of luck when buyer and seller deal directly with each other to mutual advantage. For that reason it is poor economy to try dispensing with the services of a real estate broker. A reliable one is an invaluable guide, mentor, and friend to the lamb fresh from the city. Let him know what you want and what you are willing to pay and he will do his best to find it. If a place interests you, look it over well but don't insist on so many showings that you wear out the patience of its occupants. Never, never belittle any property in the hearing of its owner. There are all too many people, cocksure but ignorant of human nature, who believe this helps to get a bargain. It works just the opposite. One would not expect to please a man by telling him that his son was wall-eyed and therefore no asset. The same man is no better pleased at hearing that his house is ugly or that the interior is something to shudder at. The prospective buyer who admits he covets the house but cannot quite meet the purchase price is much more apt to get the benefit of easier terms.

Real estate buying is still a dicker business. Get your own idea of values and then make an offer—to the broker. It is part of his job to negotiate this difference between asking and actual purchasing price. Theoretically buyer and seller should be able to meet and discuss the little matter of price in sensible and friendly fashion. Actually, there is usually as much need of a diplomat here as between two nations. One very successful broker recently admitted that he tries to keep buyer and seller apart as much as possible when negotiating the details of price, terms, concessions and the like. He stated that it is amazing how ordinarily sensible people, in the heat of a dicker over a piece of property, can get at a practical deadlock over the disposal of a cord of wood or whether a cupboard, worth possibly five dollars, is to be left with the house or removed.

So keep your temper, especially when it is a question of property you really want. We have known people who were turned aside from an ideal place for which they had hunted months, because the seller failed to fall in with some totally unimportant detail or because they didn't like something his lawyer said or the way he said it. Sellers may be cantankerous and their lawyers exasperating, but remember, you do not inherit them along with the property. Once the latter has been acquired, which is your real objective, they pass out of the picture along with your irritation at them.

In buying any property, however, make sure that the title is clear. The author of the old hymn, "When I can read my title clear to mansions in the skies," must have been familiar with the complications attendant on acquiring earthly domiciles. In other words, if the place on which you have set your heart is suffering from that obscure complaint known as a "cloudy title," it is something to be let alone unless the seller can clear it. By this term is meant that somewhere in the chain of ownership from the original land grant, some seller could not give a clear, warranted title.

There are many contributing causes for such a condition, particularly with country property in the older sections where wills and deeds were not always drawn with clarity and skill. Old second or third mortgages, presumably paid, for which satisfactions were never recorded; tax liens that have not been cleared; or possible interests of minority heirs under a will dating back a generation or more; are some of the most common causes for imperfect titles. But if one is patient and the seller is willing to cooperate, such clouds can usually be removed.

Sometimes one discovers a desirable piece of property with a cloudy title due to a family feud or the stubbornness of the present owner. Here it may be to the buyer's advantage to obtain an option on it and engage a local lawyer experienced in real estate matters to perfect the title. For example, two spinster sisters lived in their father's old farmhouse. They were not at all averse to selling, but under the terms of their father's will, a niece in a state institution for the feeble minded held a life interest in the place. Her aunts grimly refused to sell and hand over the sum representing her interest to her guardian. "Alice has cost us plenty and never been anything but a source of worry. Not a dollar more of our money goes to her as long as we live. She is in an institution where she belongs. Besides, her father was a rascal."

They were willing to sell at a price several thousand dollars less than like places in the neighborhood were bringing. So a prospective buyer negotiated an arrangement whereby he acquired an option to buy the property at this low price, provided he could make a settlement for the niece's contingent interest at his own expense. It took about six months but at last a settlement was reached through the courts. For about five hundred dollars paid to the guardian of the incompetent woman and an equal amount in court and lawyer's fees, he obtained a quit claim deed of her interest that satisfied the requirements of the corporation that was to insure the validity of the title. The day after the purchase was consummated, the new owner was offered a price for the property that would have given him a substantial profit above his investment and expenses, had he cared to sell.

Under such circumstances, however, the buyer should be sure the property is a good enough investment to be worth so much time and trouble and he should never embark on such an undertaking without the best possible legal advice. Most important of all, his contract to buy should be so drawn that ample time is allowed for the work of perfecting the title. There should also be a provision allowing him to withdraw from the contract and to regain his option money, if clearing the title proves impossible or there is too great expense.

Another detail that should be taken into account, especially with land once used for farming, is the possibility of old, half forgotten rights of way. In the legal argot, a right of way is a permission to cross property that has road frontage to reach fields, pasturage, wood lots, or the like which are otherwise without means of access. To be binding, of course, such agreements must have been recorded. Where they date back half a century and have been forgotten and unused for many years, lawyers are sometimes careless in their title search and overlook them. This is a serious omission since they can suddenly be revived to the discomfort of a totally innocent buyer.

Some years ago a man bought a simple farmhouse as a summer home. One spring he discovered that a neighbor had acquired a cow and, night and morning, was driving it across his lawn and flower garden. At his indignant protests, the neighbor sarcastically pointed out an old gateway in the stone wall dividing their property and cited an agreement almost a century old that provided for a right of way for cattle across what was now lawn and flower garden. Of course reviving this right was a case of pure spite and eventually there was a law suit. The man with the cow came to terms, his own of course, and for a cash consideration relinquished his cow driving rights. Meanwhile the owner of the property had been put to some expense and plenty of annoyance.

With the final decision to buy a piece of property financial details come to the fore. An "all cash basis" is not uncommon these days and often brings a sizable reduction in the asking price. Where a mortgage is desired, fifty per cent of the purchase price must be cash for house and land, or the entire amount on unimproved land. With the latter, the mortgage lender will expect you to provide at least half of the total cost of the land and the proposed house. Gone are the days when country homes could be bought with first and second mortgages and very little cash. This type of financing was tried and found wanting during the late depression, since it led many people to commit themselves to payments they could not continue if reverses were experienced.

There are various kinds of first mortgages now being used to assist in financing the purchase of a country home. One of the oldest is the purchase money type. This is given the seller as part of the total price paid by the buyer. Formerly such mortgages were for a short term, three or five years, and payable in full at the end of that period. Now some of them are for longer periods and provide for monthly amortization charges by which the mortgage is paid in full by the end of the time specified.

The Federal Housing Administration mortgages, which are a recent New Deal endeavor to make funds for home buying or building safe and stable, are issued by local banks with the payment of interest and principle guaranteed to the bank through the operation of this government controlled agency. These mortgages are amortized over periods of ten, fifteen, and twenty years and the borrower must make specified monthly payments that include taxes, interest charges, and amortization. They are not available in all sections because some local banks hold that they conflict in details with other banking regulations. So far as the borrower is concerned, these mortgages are no different from any other similar method of financing. If payments are not made regularly and promptly, foreclosure proceedings will be started.

Large insurance companies or savings and loan associations also issue fifteen to twenty year first mortgages, amortized over the period by monthly, quarterly, or semi-annual payments. The interest rate varies from five to five and a half per cent. If such a mortgage is arranged for a new house, architect's plans and specifications must be submitted with the application for loan. The site must be free and clear of all mortgages or other obligations. Your own financial rating is looked up by the lender and, if satisfactory, the company issues a commitment that you can take to your local bank where definite amounts are paid as the work progresses; so much when exterior walls are complete; such a proportion when rough piping for plumbing has been installed; another amount when all lath and plaster has been finished; and so on until the final payment when the house is finished. Then the formal mortgage is executed and recorded. There are brokers who specialize in negotiating such mortgages. Their fee is about two per cent.

So much for the usual channels of financing. In addition, the buyer can still make his own mortgage arrangements with some investor who has money to loan if he knows such a person. Further, although second mortgages should be avoided if possible, they are sometimes issued where a buyer is considered a good risk but lacks sufficient capital to meet the fifty per cent cash requirement that prevails today. Such loans are not usually made for over twenty per cent of the appraised value and generally call for a higher rate of interest, six per cent. They are also apt to be for a short term, two or three years, when they must be paid in full.

With both first and second mortgages, the lenders will inquire carefully into the financial responsibility of the would-be borrower. They will want to know exactly how much of his own ready money he plans to use in the transaction. This is to be sure that he has a substantial equity in the property and will not be struggling under too great a financial burden.

Having perfected the method for financing your purchase, now comes the formal contract to buy. This is an agreement whereby you undertake to consummate the purchase at a future date, generally thirty to sixty days, at the agreed price. On executing such a contract, *which should be reviewed by your lawyer before you, as buyer, sign it*, expect to pay the seller through the broker ten per cent of the total purchase price. This is done on signing the contract. The time between signing this contract and the date set for the title closing is employed for title search and insurance, land survey and similar details. If the title proves imperfect so that you cannot complete the purchase, your check is returned to you. As for the cost of title insurance, the corporations issuing such policies have an established scale of prices. These vary slightly in different parts of the country. Title policies have generally replaced the old independent title search by lawyers that had no elements of insurance. Where a company has already searched and insured the title, reissue of the policy is made to you at about half the original fee.

The cost of surveying property is based on the amount of work involved. For surveying five acres of what was formerly farm land and that has never had its borders so measured and defined, the average charge today is from one hundred to one hundred and twenty-five dollars. Special conditions may raise or lower this. An established surveyor who knows the locality is, of course, the best person to undertake such work. His previous surveys of other adjacent properties can often enable him to locate and identify old boundary marks that some one not conversant with the locality might find baffling. Much country property is very vaguely described by old deeds. "Fifty acres more or less bounded on the east by the highway, northerly by land owned by Jones, westerly to that of or recently owned by Smith, and southerly by that of Brown," illustrates roughly an old title description. You may get forty-five or fifty-five acres, and it is up to you to establish just what fences and so forth are your actual boundaries.

A surveyor reduces all this to exact measurements and puts definite markers at the corners and wherever else the party lines change direction. When finished, he provides you with a certified copy of his survey in map form, giving distances and indicating location of his monuments. These are usually either iron stakes driven two or three feet into the ground or concrete posts about two inches square set in the ground and plainly visible. It is illegal to move such marks.

With title clear and the survey completed, everything is ready for the title closing, as lawyers call the time when title to the property passes from seller to buyer. The latter's lawyer should have investigated and passed on all steps prior to this and adjusted any minor details with the seller's lawyer. The buyer and his lawyer and the seller and his lawyer should all be present at a title closing. The paid tax bills for the current year are first presented and any minor adjustments made. Then the buyer presents a certified check or actual cash for the amount he has agreed to pay. He also has a small amount of money on hand to meet any adjustments such as taxes, insurance, and the like. Lastly, the deed, which has been carefully reviewed by the buyer's lawyer, is signed by the seller and, for better or worse, you have become a country property owner.

# CHAPTER IV

## CALL IN AN ARCHITECT

The prospective country dweller is now owner of a piece of property and his ideas are probably fairly definite as to how his home is going to look when his family is actually living there. But seldom is it a simple matter of gathering the household goods into a moving van, having them set down in the new place, and then going out on the terrace to watch the sunset while deft workers within set things to rights.

There may be no house at all on his new holding, much less a terrace. At the time of purchase, an old mill, barn or other combination of walls and roof may stand in place of his imaginary home. Even a house in good condition usually needs a little renovation. During the negotiations for purchase, his lawyer kept him from legal pitfalls. Just as important now in bridging the gap between what he has and what he wants is an architect.

If he has been consulted before purchase, so much the better. If not, it is high time to seek him out unless one happens to be a genius like Thomas Jefferson who could draft a Declaration of Independence with one hand and design a serpentine wall with the other. Such a person has no need of this book anyway and will long since have cast it aside. Most of us are just average citizens with some ideas which we want to put into concrete form but find difficult because we are either inarticulate or untrained.

That is what various specialists are for, and it is a wise man who realizes his own limitations. A sugar broker may have ideas about a portrait but he won't try to paint it himself. He will commission a portrait painter, in whom he has confidence, to make a likeness of his wife or child as the case may be. Even more necessary are the services of an architect when building or remodeling a house. Trying to be your own architect is as foolish as drawing a sketch of little Jerry on canvas and then calling in a house painter to smear on a daub of blue for his coat, a bit of yellow for his hair, white for his collar, and just anything for the background. At worst, though, this futuristic result can be taken to the attic, turned face to the wall and forgotten; but a botched house won't let you forget. You have to live in it along with your mistakes, day after day and, possibly, year after year. When and if you finally call in an architect and have them remedied or obviated, the cost will be considerably in excess of what his total fee would have been in the beginning.

So, find the best man practicing in the vicinity where your future home is to be located and cast your burdens on his drafting board. Give him ample information as to what suits your fancy and conforms to your family needs. Then he can proceed with the preliminary sketches. From these eventually will come the plan of action to be followed by the various artisans who will do the work. But house plans, whether for new construction, remodeling or renovating, do not spring from the drafting board complete and final overnight. They are based on more preliminary effort than most people without building experience realize.

This is particularly true of the country home. In cities and suburbs, building plots are more or less standardized units in a checker-board with two controlling factors, so many feet of street frontage and such and such depth. Local building ordinances sharply limit the type and size of structure. The country offers much greater latitude. Such matters as topography, location of existing trees, and points of the compass with relation to the main rooms of the house play important roles.

We well remember a dismal example of what can happen when these controlling factors are ignored. The owner was an opinionated man with a passion for economy. House building was to him no mystery. It was just foundations, side walls, roof, stairways, interior partitions and, of course, plumbing, heating and so forth. His house was "going to cost just so much and people who paid architects' fees for plans had more money than brains." Besides, he had seen a sketch and floor plans of a house in a magazine that were good enough for him. He knew a builder who could follow them and what more did one need?

The little matter of relating the structure to the site concerned him not at all, nor did it enter his head that a house could face anywhere except towards the road. As for the contractor, it was not for him to reason why, but to build. So they went to work and a house entirely made up of good things done in the wrong way was the result. An outcropping of rock meant expensive blasting, so the magazine-pictured house was set firmly down almost on the roots of a fine row of old pine trees by the roadside. Through these the wind howled mournfully at night and by day their shade made the main rooms of the ground floor distinctly gloomy.

**A REALLY EARLY AMERICAN INTERIOR. THE GREAT FIREPLACE OF THE WAYSIDE INN, SUDBURY, MASS.**

*Henry Ford*

It was an ambitious house and the leaded glass windows of the living room faced north. So keeping its temperature at a comfortable point in winter was an added difficulty. The sunny southwestern exposure, being at the back, was given over to kitchen and servants' quarters. Lastly, the one pleasing prospect, a friendly little valley with a meandering brook, could only be seen to advantage from the garage. The architect's fee had been saved but when, a little later, the owner wanted to sell, it took several years to find a buyer and then only at a price of half the money invested. The new owner consulted an architect with a gift for rearranging and so succeeded in mitigating the worst features and in taking advantage of the cheerful aspects inherent with the site. Like a good doctor or lawyer, an able architect can usually get you out of trouble; but the ancient slogan, "An ounce of prevention is worth a pound of cure," fits admirably here.

Do not, however, engage an architect as lightly as you would select a cravat. To him you are intrusting the task of putting your chaotic and half-expressed thoughts and desires into a set of plans that will guide and control masons, carpenters, plumbers, electricians, and painters in their work. As your professional adviser, it will be his job to bridge the gap between the date of purchase and the happy occasion when your household goods are deposited in a home embodying your ideas and wishes.

Obviously he must be in sympathy with those ideas. If you are building a new house on old lines or remodeling an existing structure with a century or more to its credit, don't select a man to advise you who can see nothing but the newest and most modernistic types of architecture. Don't be afraid to ask for evidences of past performances. Since no architect discards his plans and renderings, he will be glad to show you a few of them. Also in this initial conference, names of clients for whom he has executed commissions within the fairly recent past may be mentioned. It is sensible to consult two or three of these. If he has pleased them, he is probably fitted to undertake your problems. For solving them and knowing how to get desired results, you will pay him a fee that ranges from six to ten per cent of the total cost of the work undertaken. For special cases that involve unusual work, it may be slightly higher. The amount of the fee, as well as the dates at which portions of it become payable, will be settled in your initial interview.

There are occasional men, however, calling themselves architects who are not qualified. They have no degree from a recognized school; cannot qualify for registration in states where architects, like doctors, lawyers, teachers and other professional people, must have a state license to practice. Like other charlatans, such men are glib talkers but it takes real ability and thorough training to prepare practical plans and specifications. Here is where the dabster betrays himself. A little independent investigation may prevent you from putting your building problems into the hands of such an incompetent man.

The need of an architect where a new house is to be built or an old one completely remodeled is obvious. We are convinced that the same holds true where only minor changes, replacements and the introduction of modern conveniences are the program. Our own little country home is an example. The necessary alterations were so simple that it seemed ridiculous to ask architectural advice. There was nothing to the job but to install plumbing, move one partition, patch the plastering, and close chimney and other pipe openings cut in the days when stoves, rather than fireplaces, furnished heat.

We engaged a good local man who, with his crew of four or five helpers, was accustomed to doing everything from carpentry to plumbing. His labor charges were on a per diem basis and considerably under the union scale that then prevailed. Nothing was left indefinite. We understood exactly how the work was to be done and what materials we were to supply. In due time it was finished and we moved in. Two or three years later, we discovered some serious shortcomings. For instance, the kitchen sink was hung in the wrong place and, because it was easier, all of the water pipes were placed on outside walls. This made no difference when the house was occupied only during the summer months but during the first winter we became experts in thawing pipes that "caught" whenever the temperature dropped to zero.

There was another economy that proved quite the opposite even before the work was finished. We had agreed that wherever the old lath and plaster were in bad condition, they were to be removed and replaced with a paper wall board then being widely advertised as an inexpensive substitute. But we had reckoned without the idiosyncrasies of an 18th century house. When the old lath and plaster had been cleared away, our handyman contractor discovered that the old beams and uprights were spaced at eighteen-inch intervals, while our new wall board came in widths conforming to the sixteen-inch spacing that has been standard with American house construction for a century. It was too late to return the wall board so new nailing strips, sixteen inches apart, had to be installed. This took time and when the so-called inexpensive substitute was finally in place, the total cost actually exceeded that of the more satisfactory lath and plaster.

Further, because nobody was at hand to prevent it, we lost a good partition of feather-edge boarding. It was between two of the bedrooms, concealed beneath several layers of wallpaper. When stripped, two or three cracks were found through which one could look from one room to the other. These could have been filled with wooden shims but the workmen did not stop to think of that. They ripped it out and put in a tight and modest partition of that ultra-modern wall board. It was well done mechanically and is still in place, but we mourn that original paneling of native white wood and continually keep an eye out for some like it.

Eventually, when all the mistakes of ignorance and lack of supervision have been corrected, we will have spent several times the total of the architect's fee. So we are out of pocket and, except for relocating the water piping, we are still looking at and repenting most of the results of our false economy.

Thus, an architect is all-important with a house problem whether it involves a minor or major undertaking and it is logical to ask exactly what he does for his fee. Consider, for instance, his functions and services when a new house is to be built. As a beginning, owner and architect meet, inspect the site, while the architect, like any good diagnostician, asks questions. These deal with the type of house the owner thinks he wants, the number of rooms, baths, and so forth and, finally, the amount of money he is prepared to spend. He offers few opinions of his own at this interview but rather tries to read his client's mind so that preliminary sketches and plans will approximate that mental picture.

A few days later, tentative sketches of a house designed to suit the location are submitted. Out of them grow the revised ones. It is highly improbable that his initial suggestions will suit you in every detail. It takes time and interchange of ideas before this can be accomplished. When they reach the stage where they represent the house you want, the architect prepares a complete set of working drawings, including floor plans and side wall elevations. These are drawn on a scale of one quarter of an inch to the foot. As soon as the drawings are finished, he drafts the specifications or bill of particulars as to materials to be used in the construction of the house. These with the plans form the basis on which contractors may submit bids for the work.

First, however, owner and architect should go over this material together. Making changes after the contracts are let and the work begun is both expensive and foolish. If you find it difficult to visualize an actual house from the drawings, a model made from wall board or similar material is a wise precaution. Fashioned on the same scale of one quarter of an inch to the foot, it is your proposed house in the little, and on seeing it no doubts are left. Windows and doors are all in their proper places. The exterior is painted to match the color and simulate the material that is to be used. Finally, the model can be taken apart so that you can study the interior of bedroom and living room floors. Such models, of course, are not included in the architect's fee but the cost of one for an average house is under $100. If you can visualize your proposed home thoroughly by it, the expense is well warranted.

The architect can be of great service in the matter of contractor's bids. He knows the past performances of those operating in the vicinity where you propose building and can suggest the men or firms whose work is most satisfactory. From four to eight general contractors, that is, individuals or firms competent to undertake the complete building operation, ought to be invited to submit sealed bids. Each is supplied with a complete set of plans and specifications by the architect and given from ten days to two weeks in which to submit their bids. In addition to the total price for the work, these bids, by common custom, give the names of the chief sub-contractors such as plumber, electrician and the like, with the amount of money allocated for the work of each.

On a set day, usually a Saturday afternoon, owner and architect meet, open the bids, and compare the offers made by the various contractors. Most of them include alternate provisions on condition that they be allowed to substitute materials or methods of construction not according to the specifications. The contractor who submits the lowest bid would logically be the one selected but here again the architect's judgment is valuable. First, he can rapidly determine whether the provisional saving suggested by substitution of unspecified materials is a wise change. Second, he knows whether the bidder under consideration is dependable or inclined to skimp in hidden but essential points.

There is, also, the possible chance that none of the bids submitted come within the sum the owner is prepared to spend. Then comes the task of revising plans and specifications and eliminating non-essentials to bring costs within the set figure. From practical experience, however, architects have found that, if the proposed house is just what the owner wants, he will somehow find the additional money rather than have plans or details changed.

After a contractor whose bid and quality of work are satisfactory has been selected, the architect, acting for the owner, lets the contract to him. This includes provisions for partial payments at stated periods as the work progresses; so much when the masonry is completed; another amount when the exterior walls are finished; and so on, including plumbing, heating, plastering and electrical wiring. With each payment, fifteen per cent of the total is held back and does not become due until the entire work has been finished. This is a standard practice and is intended to insure completion of the contract to the satisfaction of both owner and architect. Under this provision, the architect certifies to the owner each month that certain work has been done and that the contractor is entitled to so much money for it.

From the day that construction starts, the architect begins his work of supervision. At least twice a week he goes to the site and observes the progress of the work and how it is being done. Special conditions may arise where the contractor or his foreman call hurriedly for the architect, such as uncovering a large boulder at one corner of the excavation for the cellar. There may be a fine point to be decided regarding the location of piping or some detailed instruction concerning the installation of the interior woodwork. On these occasions it saves time for everybody if the architect or one of his associates is readily available. Watching the cellar excavation for unexpected subsurface water is also an item that no experienced architect neglects. He sees to it that concrete for foundations is mixed properly and has the specified percentage of cement. The installation of piping for plumbing and heating is supervised carefully, as is the work of plastering.

As the house nears completion, his supervision increases in direct ratio. In fact, during the last two or three weeks, the architect is not infrequently there most of the time. The last details of the interior trim are being completed, decorating is under way, and lighting fixtures are being installed. All of these require direct supervision and the architect expects to be on hand. These final details can make or mar the general effect more than is realized.

When your house is finished to the architect's satisfaction, he gives his final approval and thirty days thereafter the final bill of the contractor is payable. This period is to allow for minor adjustments, such as windows that stick, doors that will not latch and the like, the small things that always need to be done with any new house and are generally attended to after the owner and his family have taken possession.

Just as the general contractor is paid in installments, the architect's fee is likewise liquidated. There is a standard schedule which provides that one-fifth of the estimated fee shall be paid on completion of satisfactory preliminary sketches; two-fifths when the plans and specifications are finished or on letting the contract for actual building. The balance is paid monthly in proportion to the amounts paid the contractor.

When a house is to be remodeled, the architect proceeds in much the same way. He presents suggested sketches of the ways in which the desired changes can be accomplished. When these are satisfactory, working drawings are prepared that show what is to be removed and what new construction undertaken. The working drawings are, of course, accompanied by a set of specifications, and contractors are invited to submit bids for doing the work. On letting the contract, work proceeds about as with that of building a new house. There are, however, more opportunities for unforeseen contingencies and so the architect often has to devote more of his time to supervision. Sometimes, if the particular remodeling project is one requiring unusual care, the percentage of his fee is a little higher by special arrangement.

Where a house requires minor changes that qualify merely as renovation, the architect's work is, of course, much simpler. Extensive preliminary sketches are unnecessary, and complete floor and elevation plans not required. But architectural investigation, planning and supervision, as stated before, are highly desirable if not essential. His fee is usually the same ten per cent as applies for new construction. There is less actual plan drafting but the amount of supervision is so much in excess of that required for new construction that such a charge is by no means unreasonable. Besides, the owner has the assurance that all changes and new installations will be done properly with no glaring errors of judgment to mock him as he settles down to life in his country home.

# CHAPTER V

## BUILDING VERSUS REMODELING

"Shall I build or remodel?" is a question with so many facets that it would be foolhardy to try to answer it categorically. Circumstances alter cases in all phases of life and particularly so when one is endeavoring to decide whether the country home is to be a new structure, or an old one remodeled to make the best use of its desirable features and suit the requirements of its new owner.

One of our acquaintances was hung on the horns of this dilemma for several months while he and his wife spent most of their waking hours arguing it pro and con. They had selected the vicinity in which they wanted to live, had the requisite cash in the bank to finance either undertaking, and there were two properties that pleased them. The latter constituted the snag. On the one hand, there was a sightly piece of land with some nice old shade trees but no existing structure; about a mile farther along the same road, lay another holding of about the same size with a house in fair condition. The price for this was naturally higher than for the undeveloped land, on the theory that it would not cost half as much to remodel the house as to build.

"I don't know what to do," this perplexed man remarked. "On one side I hear and read that new building is much the best investment. That it costs so much less to maintain a new house and if you want to sell, you can find a purchaser quicker and at a better price. But no sooner do I begin to believe that building is the only wise course, than I run smack into an article on remodeling or meet some one I know whose experience in remodeling shows by actual figures a big saving compared with a new house of the same kind and size. In my own case, though, the more I study what estimates I can get, the more I am convinced that in the end I'll spend just about as much whether I build or remodel."

These two people finally built a new house. There were good reasons for their decision. First, they could buy the land for so much money, and a general contractor of excellent reputation was ready to build just the house they wanted for so much more. The two figures, plus the architect's fee, added up to a definite amount. Having an accounting mind, the knowledge that there would be no unforeseen contingencies and that, ready for occupancy, the cost of the house would be so much, was the deciding factor. In addition, he and his wife both inclined towards something new. A house that had not been lived in by other people, had no scars and marks of age and use, that embodied all the newest materials and construction methods, was really what they wanted. Had remodeling offered them an assured saving of several thousand dollars, this couple would probably have suppressed their subconscious leanings to be builders, proceeded to remodel, and been only moderately pleased with the result.

The answer to the age-old question of whether to build or to remodel is found in the preference of the individual. Some people are temperamentally builders. They are happiest living in a home that was constructed for them. In their eyes it possesses far greater charm than anything that has been mellowed by years of use. There are others to whom nothing is more satisfying than to take an existing structure and alter it to their liking and needs. An elderly acquaintance, now a widow and living in a sleepy New England village, is taking keen pleasure in an old house of almost doll-like proportions. "All my life," she said, "I've wanted to live in a really old house but until now it has always been one new house or city apartment after another and I never got my roots down."

Granted that building or remodeling, like cheese, is a matter of personal preference, it is not improper at this point to set forth some of the merits of both. With a fine old building, there is that elusive something called charm. Time has mellowed it and the countless feet that have crossed its threshold have worn its floors. The blackened bricks or stones of its fireplaces bespeak the generations that basked in the heat of the huge logs that once glowed there. All these things have given it character.

Don't expect a new house, the day it is turned over to you by the contractor, to look as if it had been a family home for several generations. It can't. It has just been built. Everything is fresh and shiny; edges are sharp and even the bricks of the fireplace are untainted by flame and smoke. But if you have been even moderately articulate, the architect has been able to interpret your wishes and you have a house built as near as possible to your plans. You also have the satisfaction of knowing that, in the building, the workmanship has been honest and thorough, and that in materials used every advantage has been taken of the newest developments.

**ONCE HALF A HOUSE AND A HEN ROOST**

*Photo by Whitney*

For instance, behind the plaster is the modern metal lath so superior to the old wooden variety. The exterior walls are as thoroughly insulated against heat and cold as any one of several highly efficient materials can make them; windows and doors are products of large wood-fabricating factories noted for superior work. All these are points of advantage with tangible merit, but time and your own efforts are the only means by which your new home can acquire personality and charm. This new structure is yours, made to your desires; and what you make of it is your own problem.

**WHAT CAN BE DONE WITH A BARN**

*Photo by Samuel H. Gottscho. Robertson Ward, architect*

The house that you buy and remodel starts with certain attributes given by age, as already stated. Here we must offer one caution. It concerns houses built during the last quarter of the 19th century. The majority were badly designed and the quality of workmanship was none too good. Such houses are apt to be perched on high foundations, have exterior walls that offer the minimum resistance to winter winds, while architecturally, lines and proportions reflect an age when taste was either bad or lacking. We know of several attempts to remodel country homes of such vintage and are convinced that better results could have been achieved for less money if the operation had started with wrecking the structure and building anew.

On the contrary, except where decayed beyond salvage, we have yet to see a country home of the 18th or first half of the 19th century that did not respond admirably to remodeling. But it is well to be practical and compare its cost with that of a new building. Among architects, it is generally recognized that, save for a house with unusually expensive details or added equipment, definite figures per cubic foot of size may be computed that will cover the entire cost of construction. To get the cubical contents of a house, the architect takes the area in square feet of the ground floor and multiplies it by the height from the cellar floor to the eaves, plus half the distance from that point to the ridge of the roof.

For example, if the proposed house is thirty feet wide by twenty feet deep, its floor plan area is 600 square feet. Then, if the elevation dimensions are seven feet from cellar floor to living room floor; eight feet from living room floor to that of the bedroom floor; and seven feet from bedroom floor to the level of the eaves, which in turn measure eight feet below the ridge of the roof; the cubical contents would result from multiplying 600 square feet by the sum of seven, eight, seven, and four, or 15,600 cubic feet. With this figure established, it is simple to approximate costs as follows:

| | | |
|---|---|---|
| Wooden construction | $0.45 | per cubic foot |
| Brick veneer construction | 0.55 | per cubic foot |
| Solid brick construction | 0.65 | per cubic foot |
| Field stone construction | 0.60 | per cubic foot |
| Cut stone construction | $0.75 to 1.50 | per cubic foot |

This tabulation, an average for the United States as a whole, is as accurate as any generalization can be and a safe one for forming a preliminary estimate, but local conditions may increase or decrease costs. The architect can readily determine which. This table, of course, does not include cost of land, construction of driveway, landscaping, or expenses incident to bringing electric service or telephone wires to the house.

From these calculations, it is an easy matter to take the outside dimensions of a house you are considering remodeling and compute its cubical content. Then you can ask your architect whether it can be remodeled as you wish for a price competitive with building a new house of like design and equal size. In order for this to mean anything, you should determine what proportion of the price paid for the property represents land value and what reflects the existence of the structure itself. As a simple example, we will concede that land in the neighborhood is held at $500 an acre and you can buy a five-acre tract with a house on it for $3,750. Here $2,500 represents land value, and $1,250 house value. The question resolves itself into comparing remodeling costs plus house value with those for a new house of like size and kind.

If so much must be replaced or rearranged that the figures for house and remodeling are in excess of those for a new structure, the wise course would be to abandon the idea and build instead. But the old house may have certain details that make you willing to bear the added expense. If so, you at least know the comparative costs and have definite standards by which to shape your course.

From personal observation, we believe that there are many instances where the total cost of house and rejuvenation is considerably below that of a new structure. Since confession stories are just as fascinating in home building as in the lurid fiction of the woodpulp magazines, we cite the experience of a family that bought a home nearly two years ago within the New York commuting zone. They were a larger family than the average and the house, of desired size, had once been a stagecoach halfway tavern. It contained twenty-two rooms and was in better than average condition. The exterior had been given two coats of white paint less than six months before.

The price for this old place, including twenty-two acres of land and a barn usable for garage and chicken house, was $8,200. According to actual record, only $2,798 was spent on remodeling. There were almost no structural changes required. Two minor partitions were removed and five new windows cut. Otherwise, this expenditure was largely devoted to the introduction of plumbing, heating, and lighting. By type of work, the costs for this remodeling were as follows:

| | |
|---|---|
| Two bathrooms, each complete with shower; a kitchen sink and laundry tub | $590.00 |
| Heating system, including steam boiler, piping and 25 radiators, totaling 630 feet of radiation | 889.00 |
| Water system, cleaning well, installing pump and 500 gallon storage tank | 218.00 |
| Electric wiring entirely of armored cable and lighting fixtures | 306.00 |
| Sewage system complete with septic tank and disposal fields | 230.00 |
| All carpentry, including necessary work for plumber, electrician, etc. | 160.00 |
| Masonry, including repairs to fireplaces and chimneys | 105.00 |
| Decorations, paint, and paper for twelve rooms | 150.00 |
| Architectural supervision, plans where needed and preliminary inspection of several houses | 150.00 |
| **Total** | $2,798.00 |

These are the actual figures for a livable and attractive country home. There are, of course, some things that await a future time for their accomplishment, but what place would be really enjoyable if there were not certain corrections and additions over which the owners could daydream and plan. We admit the figures just quoted are so low as to seem hardly credible, but they demonstrate what could be accomplished within fifty miles of New York during the summer of 1935. The contributing causes for this happy result were that these people knew what they wanted, hunted in a section that had not been too thoroughly combed by others like themselves and, lastly, happened to be ready to buy at just the right moment when the man who owned the property was anxious to sell.

But old country residences, including structures built as taverns, private schools and the like, are not the only type of buildings that may be remodeled into acceptable homes. We have seen old barns or stables, disused sawmills, general stores, old stone buildings that once housed small industrial enterprises, and even a church of the Neo-Classic period remodeled with distinct success.

Again, in Massachusetts there is a former textile hamlet. The mill itself is now a community club and the workmen's cottages, built about 1815-20, are homes for a dozen or more families where, daily, the head of the house motors to his office in an industrial city about a half-hour away. These story-and-a-half cottages, executed along simple Federal lines, are owned by the families who occupy them. They look out on a street lined with fine old elms and at the end is the stone mill with its belfry where still hangs the bell that once ruled the lives of spinners and weavers with its clanking iron tongue, morning, noon and night.

For picturesqueness, if the unconventional has a greater appeal than the more standardized type of home, remodeling an old barn into a country home has its advantages. This is particularly so if one can find either a capacious one of roughly laid ledge stone, once popular in parts of New Jersey and Pennsylvania and more rarely built in other sections, or a large hay barn with hand-hewn framework and side walls of weathered boarding. It takes only a little imagination to visualize such a building remodeled into a country home with a generous stone chimney and fireplace occupying one of the end walls of a former haymow. Invariably such remodeling includes construction of one or more wings to house dining room, kitchen, and servants' quarters as well as additional bedrooms and baths. The actual barn structure seldom lends itself to more than a living room and possibly two bedrooms.

In summer this type of country home has much to offer. It is light, airy, and spacious; but when fall begins to indicate its arrival, unless the structure has been made nearer weather tight than is the nature of barns, life in the haymow is chill and sour. For use the year around, the old barn must be completely rebuilt with a cellar beneath for a heating plant and side walls and undersides of roof well covered with insulating material to prevent cold from entering or heat escaping. One of the most successful methods of treating the front, where once the old barn doors swung wide to admit a fully loaded haywagon, is to substitute a many-paned window of almost cathedral proportions. This lets in adequate light for what might otherwise be a dark interior. In summer it can be screened to keep out flies and mosquitoes. Through it on fair winter days, especially if it faces south or west, pours that most valuable attribute of country living, bright sunlight.

An old water-power sawmill makes an unusually attractive country home. We know of at least one so adapted. Here the space once given over to sawing logs into boards has been completely enclosed and is now the living room. On one side is a noble fireplace flanked by large casement windows that look out on the old mill pond. Bedrooms and service quarters are located in the end sections where lumber used to be seasoned and other special work done. This unique bit of remodeling, combined with the pond as a main feature of landscape development, is both rare and enviable. Yet there are a surprising number of old commercial structures that lend themselves to remodeling into present day homes and by their very unconventionality take on added charm.

In New England there is a substantial stone building of no architectural pretensions except that width, depth, and height are distinctly related to each other. It is now a country home but it began as a small textile mill in the early days of the 19th century when the industrial revolution was just getting under way. Later, when the factory era became thoroughly established, this lone little mill was left high and dry by the tide that swept toward the larger centers and it stood untenanted for years. Finally it was retrieved by some one with vision enough to see that, with proper partitions, both ground and second floors could be divided into satisfactory rooms. Here the new owner, or his architect, had the discretion to preserve as much as possible of the past. The old mill owner's counting room, on the lower floor, is now the library and, in almost untouched condition, is complete even to the cast-iron stove that once warmed it.

Converting buildings originally designed for other uses may take a still different course. A house, too small in itself for present day use, can form the nucleus of a country home. A most attractive place in Maine was so assembled. There were two or three other buildings on the property which were shifted from their original locations by jacks and rollers and skillfully joined to the little house to form wings. By clever rearrangement of rooms and shifting or removal of partitions, the assembled group became large enough for the new owner's uses.

Even a modern structure, designed originally for some branch of agriculture, can be converted into an excellent house if an architect is inclined to undertake the necessary contriving of plans and builders can be found who will follow his directions. Several years ago, a man was bitten with the urge to raise chickens according to the latest scientific methods of artificial lighting and forced feeding. For this he built a substantial structure with steam heat, electric lights, and other elaborate provisions. Being nurse maid to thousands of chicks ranging from a week old to the proper size for broiling was a strenuous job. Further, the creatures developed all sorts of maladies not provided for in the book and the mortality was so high that the project was finally abandoned.

The building stood vacant for some months until it came to the notice of a resourceful young architect. He measured, sketched, and drew plans. Now, what was once a factory for the raw material of broiled chicken is an attractive and compact Cape Cod cottage. Because of site and accessibility, the original building had to be dismembered and moved about two hundred feet. When re-erected according to the plans provided, the result bore little resemblance to the original box-like structure except that the floor space was the same.

Some country homes begin as week-end retreats. Then the habit of being in the country two or three days grows on the family until they see no reason for living in the city except for an occasional overnight ordeal with a stuffy hotel room. To make the average week-end shack a permanent home calls for material expansion. Double-deck bunks have been installed to provide adequate sleeping quarters; and for a limited time they find it fun to cook, eat, and live in one large room. But, when the house is used seven days a week, such condensation is anything but practical. So the establishment must be enlarged. This can be done with ease, especially if the original plans were drawn with such a change in mind. That is, the original structure now becomes the living room, while new wings and additions provide the much needed space for service quarters and conventional bedrooms and baths.

But the week-end place is not always built particularly for the purpose. Many times it is a very small farmhouse acquired cheaply and made usable at a minimum of time and money. When the decision is reached to convert it into a home of larger proportions, whether one realizes it or not, the plan of campaign follows the plan of no less a person than George Washington. Mount Vernon was not always a mansion but was the result of consistent enlargement. When Washington inherited it from his half-brother, Lawrence, it was a story-and-a-half hunting lodge of eight rooms. Then he married Martha Custis, richest widow in the Virginia colony; and, to have a home suitable for her, he had the roof raised and the house made full two stories.

Shortly before the outbreak of the American Revolution, he planned two wings. The first was that at the south end with library on the ground floor and master bedroom for Colonel and Mrs. Washington on the second. As the revolt against the British crown progressed, the construction of the north wing lagged somewhat but was worked on intermittently. This, the banquet hall, when finished became one of the noblest private residence rooms in America.

Washington, however, did not leave these steps in the enlargement and renovation of his erstwhile hunting lodge entirely to professionals. Whether away fighting in the French and Indian Wars or directing the course of action of the Continental Army, he never forgot what was happening at his country seat. His correspondence is full of minute directions regarding the finishing of certain rooms or of such injunctions as, "I beg of you to hasten Lamphire about the addition to the north end of the house; otherwise you will have it open, I fear, in the cold and wet weather." When the Revolution was fought and won, the Washingtons returned, not to a Mount Vernon that was a stranger to them, but to the country home they had so carefully planned. This specific planning by the owner, now as then, has definite bearing on whether the house will be yours or just a beautiful structure, perfect in all its appointments but totally lacking the impress of the owner or his family.

Several years ago, a man and his wife acquired one of the early Dutch farmhouses of the New Jersey back country. They had long wanted just such a place and having taken possession, they summoned an architect, an interior decorator, and a landscape architect. A few days were spent with them inspecting house and grounds. Then the new owners left on a winter cruise around the world. Their final injunctions were to the effect that next May they would return and would expect everything done. They did and everything was complete. The old house was perfect. Its furnishings were all genuine antiques of the period. The grounds had been graded, trimmed, and polished. Gardens, shrubbery, and hedges were just right, but the final effect was as impersonal as a demonstration model.

In a year or two, this property was sold to a golf club and its former owner bought another place and moved right in. Nearly two years were spent consulting and working with an architect and workmen, supervising a garden or two, and in buying antiques, a piece at a time. His second attempt at country living was not as sophisticated nor did it approach the museum standards of the former; but, when completed, it had that prime essential of any home, it reflected the character and personality of its owners.

# CHAPTER VI

## LOOKING AN OLD HOUSE IN THE MOUTH

Buying an old house is a good deal like selecting a horse. Having found an animal of the desired type and breed, the question arises, "Is it sound of wind and limb?" Houses nearing or past the century mark also have their spavins and these should be recognized by the prospective buyer. He can thus form some estimate of how extensive replacements are needed, even on first inspection. This is of prime importance since it has direct bearing on the worth of the house.

Whether built of stone, brick, or wood, such structures may have rafters, sills, and main beams so decayed that new ones must be added. The foundation may need rebuilding and door and window frames may be so weathered that they also must be replaced. Beware of a house where floors slope and side walls are out of plumb. This means extensive shoring which is slow and expensive.

For a truly pessimistic report on the health of an old place turn to a trusted carpenter or contractor. He congenitally dislikes old buildings and will point out all defects with ominous head shakings and subtle suggestions for new building. In this way the prospective buyer will know the worst, painted at its blackest. Somewhere between it and the rosy view of the real estate agent will lie the truth. Therefore, it is well to do some inspecting independently. Knowledge of what are the weak spots in old houses and where to look for them will save much time and effort in the initial stages of house hunting.

The skeleton of an old house is akin to that of a modern steel structure. Hand-hewn timbers, morticed and pinned together, take the place of riveted steel beams. Since a timber frame is subject to rot, either dry or damp, one of the first places to look for unsoundness is the sills (the beams which rest on the foundation and into which are set floor joists, corner posts, and other main uprights). It is a simple matter to give them the jack-knife test at intervals of two or three feet. Stick the blade in as far as possible. Then try to turn it around. With a sound beam this cannot be done. If there is dry rot, the beam will often crumble under a slight pressure of the fingers.

Go over the sills on the north side of the building first. Here there is less sunlight and snow remains longer. Consequently decay from excessive moisture is not unusual. Roof rafters and plate beams (the long timbers on which the lower ends of the rafters rest) should also be knife-tested since long neglected leaking roofs eventually result in their decay. Unsound corner posts and other uprights connecting sills and plate beams are harder to detect since they are concealed between the outside boarding and interior plaster. Note the walls themselves and the corner boards extending vertically from foundation to eaves. If a corner of the house is enough out of plumb to be visible to the eye, or if the corner boards are loose, examine further as it may indicate decay beneath.

With brick or stone houses, the walls themselves carry the weight of the roof and so have no vertical timbers. If the walls are out of plumb it means that the foundations are either gone or are in need of major repair. Whether a house is of brick, stone or wood, there is one further place for knife testing—the ground floor joists. Cellar dampness may have taken its toll.

The fact that a sill, joist or other timber is unsound does not mean that the house is beyond repair. Many old houses with all their sills gone and some other principal beams no longer serviceable have been restored, but the necessity of such steps ought to be realized in advance and the cost taken into consideration. It is far from pleasant to discover that one has unwittingly bought the bill of expense this type of replacement means. "Let the buyer beware" generally rules in the selling of old places, and the purchase of a knife and an hour or two of poking its point into the principal timbers may save time and money later.

"The next time I buy an old house to put a new frame into, you'll know it," was the heartfelt declaration of a man who left his knife at home when he went house hunting. "The owner and the agent knew the sills and beams were rotten but didn't think it necessary to mention the fact. What I didn't see wouldn't hurt me until after I had bought the place and begun repairs. Then I learned plenty about decayed timbers and the cost of replacing them."

After the timber frame, consider the exterior. The foundation will probably need some "pointing-up," that is, replacement of mortar in the joints or cracks. The question is, how much? Will it have to be a complete job? Has frost worked such havoc that some sections must be re-laid?

If the cellar indicates standing water during heavy rains, drainage must be provided. Notice whether any cellar windows have been closed. Countrymen are prone to do this as a cheap and easy method when the framework gets beyond repair. Replacing stoned-up windows is not expensive or difficult but just one more thing which must be done. Notice the extent of the cellar. Old builders sometimes did only a partial job of excavation because of economy. Such a cellar was ample for storing root crops, preserves, and hard cider in the days before furnaces. It may be wise to complete the work of excavating. Do not expect to find cellars under wings and sheds. It was never the practice. If they are to be converted to uses for which excavation is desirable, this is another item for the adding machine.

With the foundation and its needed repairs noted, begin appraising the condition of the walls and roof. Sometimes a shingle roof will be found in good order or at most have one or two minor leaks which can be repaired. More often an entire new roof is needed and, in extreme cases, new boarding beneath. As with sills, roofs sloping to the north and east are more apt to be out of repair and for the same reasons.

If door and window frames are so loose that they can be lifted out of the side walls, the situation is serious. Putty and paint are of no avail. Rebuilding them is essential. It is extravagant business trying to heat a house with wind whistling in around doors and windows.

If the fabric of the side walls is of shingle, clapboard, or other types of wood, is the material sound enough to warrant repainting or must it be renewed? The object of paint is to close the small cracks and preserve the wood. An old house that has gone many years without painting will absorb much more than a new one, but it is surprising what can be accomplished with two or three coats of paint on siding so weathered as to seem worthless. Besides, a new exterior robs an old house of some of its charm, so preserve the old if possible, architects, carpenters, and contractors to the contrary.

Where walls are of stone or brick, the mortar of the joints has probably so disintegrated under wind and rain that repointing is indicated. Also, frosts may have heaved individual stones or disintegrated bricks so they must be reset. Expect this in places where down-spouts have leaked for years. If the walls have settled badly, lintels or sills of doors and window openings may be cracked and need renewing. Sometimes an old house has exterior walls of plaster. These are both picturesque and rare. Patch cracks and spots where it has come loose from the lath. Old plaster has a texture and patina that modern stucco cannot simulate, so preserve it if possible.

Indoors, there are many things to be observed and appraised but fireplaces come first. A country home without facilities for open fires is as uninviting as one without trees and flowers. Expect to find the fireplaces disused and closed with fireboards or bricks. Sometimes the mantels have been removed and new flooring laid over the hearthstones. Some detective work around the logical locations will tell whether fireplaces have been torn out or just concealed. If mantels are missing, look for them in the attic or on the rafters of a shed. More than one fine old mantel has been rescued from such a hiding place. We know of one fireplace complete with crane and iron cooking utensils that reposed for fifty years or more behind an unsuspected opening covered with lath and plaster.

Where original fireplaces have been torn out and chimneys intended only to serve stoves put in place, two courses are open. The more costly is rebuilding chimney and fireplaces according to indications of original dimensions. The alternative is a Franklin stove, a combination of stove and fireplace, which can be installed and connected to the existing chimney at a very moderate expense.

Incidentally, the chimneys of an old house should be examined carefully. Built in the days before separate flues and flue tiles, their mortar may have lost its binding strength and so a smoke test is advisable. Close all fireplaces except one and start a lively fire in it. When it is well under way, toss on some scraps of roofing paper. Then cover the top of the chimney. If there are any fissures in the chimney, your eyes and nose will leave you in no doubt. You cannot mistake the pungent odor of burning tar and its bluish smoke is easy to see. Trace these to the points where they leak from the chimney and mark the spots. Complete examination will tell whether repointing will suffice or whether rebuilding is necessary.

The condition of the plaster on walls and ceilings of rooms can be easily appraised. It is reasonable to expect cracks and that some of it will be so loose as to need replacing. Removing it all and starting afresh, however, is only advisable where a house has reached about the last stages of disrepair.

Partitions of even the simplest feather-board paneling should be preserved as well as interior trim, doors, and flooring. The same applies to old hardware, as a house with all original wrought-iron hinges, latches, and locks is both rare and valuable. Notice whether the floors are of old wide boards laid random width and held in place by wrought-iron nails. In houses antedating 1800, the floors in certain localities were of hardwood. Sometimes several varieties were used indiscriminately. With all their irregularities, they become a very pleasing feature when well scrubbed and oiled or waxed. Like fireplaces, they are sometimes concealed but it is an easy matter to remove the new flooring.

The soundness and safety of stairways can only be determined by direct inspection. If treads move beneath the feet, additional nailing is needed and possibly new supports. Step easily on those leading to the cellar. They are often somewhat rotten and may collapse.

If window glass is of the old, wavy, off-color sort, full of the bubbles, sand pits, and creases that characterized its production in early days, make sure that such panes are not discarded. Workmen view them with complete scorn and will cast them aside if not put under stern injunctions. "I never found that it kept out the cold any better than a good new piece," snorted one disgustedly when we suggested that he putty a fine "bull's eye" pane with a slight crack.

Sometimes part of the interior trim will have been replaced by modern substitutes, but a good carpenter working under an architect can match that still remaining. Likewise, later additions not in keeping with the original, such as porches, sheds, wings, and illogical partitions, can be readily removed with little damage to the house itself.

As one goes about an old house it is well to be on the look out for signs of vermin, both animal and insect. With the former, traps and prepared bait will suffice. The latter require the services of an exterminator or some one skilled in the use of hydrocyanic acid gas. Such insects go deep into the cracks of woodwork and beams. Ordinary fumigating will not eradicate them. A single session with this deadly gas, however, will rid the house both of these pests and their eggs.

The things that may be the matter with an old house, as enumerated here, may sound very forbidding but circumstances alter cases. It is doubtful if any one structure will be afflicted with all these ills of decay and neglect. In our own house hunting we saw many that were sound enough so that, with the addition of modern conveniences and a good cleaning, they were livable. In fact, there is nothing equal to getting thoroughly acquainted with a house before radical changes are made. Live in the place six months or a year and then you will know better just what alterations or additions are wise.

In northern New England there is a delightful country home that has been renovated with great skill and charm. The reason behind it is that the owners went for many years with as few repairs as possible. Then came a large and unexpected inheritance. There was money enough to rebuild completely but relatively few major changes were made.

"Most of the expenditure was for restorations," the owner stated. "Once we day-dreamed of all kinds of changes but when the time came we knew most of them were impractical and would add neither to our comfort nor our convenience."

The most important thing about any house is, does it please you architecturally and is its general plan suited to your needs? If it seems to be well enough preserved so that renovation appears to be practical, turn to an architect with the understanding that, if you buy, he will be retained. He will then be willing to give the house an expert inspection and even submit tentative sketches of advantageous changes. His report, if the venture is to be financially good, should indicate that structurally the house is about one-half sound and usable.

Of course if you have found a house dating from the 17th or 18th century, you have something fairly rare and it is worth reclaiming even though very extensive replacements are needed. In Fairfield, Connecticut, for example, there is the Ogden House, built before 1710. Its present owner paid $4,000 for it in what seemed to be ruinous condition. Its renovation cost fully $12,000; but finished, this old salt box house is so unusual that more than one buyer is ready and waiting to pay double the amount spent.

Arrangement of the rooms of an old house, and how they will fit the requirements of the prospective purchaser, should be given more than passing thought. Most people when they begin looking at places have large ideas about moving partitions, cutting new windows, and changing the location of doorways. These can be done but they are relatively expensive and if carried to excess rob the place of all character. Even the simplest of old houses has definite balance in its design and arrangement of rooms. So think well before tearing out partitions indiscriminately or moving doorways and cutting windows.

In fact, if some old house seems to you to call for drastic reconstruction, you would do better to let it alone and look for one that more nearly fits your mental picture. Buying a house you do not really like is as foolish as marrying with the same reservation. Some hardy people go through life so mated but more get a divorce. So it will be with the house. After a season of dislike, divorce by sale will be the end. If it pleases you from the start, however, you and it will develop a mutual affection as the years go by and it will become the old home in more ways than one.

# CHAPTER VII

## NEW SITES FOR OLD HOUSES

Substantial houses built by old craftsmen who knew how to achieve beauty by restraint lined the straggling single street of a forgotten farming town. Despite weatherbeaten clapboards and sagging roofs, the fine ornamental detail of doorways and window frames assured similar niceties within.

"What good are they," snorted practical grandfather. "If they were where people had adequate incomes it would be different. But here! Once this was a prosperous town. Men made money breeding merino sheep. Now the town's dead and its houses falling apart. Better tear them down to save taxes."

Twenty-five years ago many substantial old houses were doomed to die with their towns. Today, people who want an old house but cannot find it where they wish to live have learned that it is practical, financially and otherwise, to transplant an old structure to a new location. Once this was the sport of eccentric millionaires or of amply endowed museums. Now it is done for people of average incomes. The expense will about equal that of building a new house of the same cubical content and architectural detail. Sometimes it can be accomplished at a slight saving. But whether the cost is equal, a little higher, or somewhat less, the great advantages of a transplanted house are a certain mellowness of age and that charm of individuality which only old structures possess.

For those who want an old house on a site of their own choosing, there are now men who deal in old buildings ready for removal. Just as pickers comb the back-country for antiques, a related group search for untenanted old houses. These men are a cross between practical builders and antique dealers. They know Early American domestic architecture and experience has taught them the point beyond which salvage is impossible. Also they are experts in dismembering such houses so they can be re-erected.

Tearing down an old house is easy enough, but to do it so that it can be rebuilt is a trade in itself. From removing paneling and interior trim to taking apart the hewn timber frame requires care and understanding. Too much brute strength will split boards that should be saved. Similarly, it is disastrous if mortice and tenon joints are sawed apart. Such are the short cuts of ignorance to be expected of ordinary carpenters and handy men. And when the old house is on the ground they will display exasperating unconcern regarding what goes where and how to put the structure back together. The most complicated jig-saw puzzle is simplicity itself compared with an Early American house taken apart without predetermined marking and numbering.

Having learned this by bitter experience, these experts have evolved marking systems that prevent confusion and follow them rigidly. Likewise, since old house lumber when taken apart and stored warps and splits so badly that it can only be used again with difficulty, they leave their houses standing wherever possible until sold. They are far from impressive in this state and it takes both imagination and enthusiasm to inspect the assortment offered. Usually the roof and possibly one or two of the sides will be covered with prosaic roofing paper. The doors and windows will be securely boarded with coarse lumber.

The depredations of nature lovers who uproot shrubbery and rend such flowering trees as dogwood are as nothing when an amateur antiquarian finds an early 18th century house unoccupied. Such enthusiasts steal and wreck like Huns. Nothing is safe from them. Door knockers, H and L hinges, fireplace cranes, wavy old window glass, whole sections of paneling and even hearthstones are wrenched from place with light-hearted abandon. What they don't make away with, they generally ruin. One visit from such a relic hunter may leave an old house a shambles. How otherwise upright people with a modicum of interest in antiques will glory in looting old houses is truly remarkable. We knew one whose pride was a collection of fireplace cranes so filched.

Knowing this, the old house dealer, immediately he has bought a structure, makes it as weather-tight and marauder-proof as possible. Sagging floors and weak stairways are braced, as are fireplaces injured by dampness and frosts. Paneled partitions are stripped of layers of disguising wall paper. Any efforts to modernize that hide original conditions are torn out and the house cleared of the rubbish left by its last tenant. Even then such a house is not overly attractive to particular housekeepers.

To offset this, the old house dealer first shows one or more albums of pictures of the houses he has for sale. These contain complete snap-shots inside and out, together with plans and dimensions. If he is wise, he also has simple typed statements, giving all the data he has been able to gather concerning each house, approximately when it was built, its connection with local historical events, and, if possible, the names of prominent personages who dwelt in it or were guests there. Knowing that buyers are much impressed by such facts, he often makes a careful search of recorded deeds and books of local history for those few interesting facts that he may use advantageously. For instance, to be able to say that Lafayette, on his extensive old-age visit to the United States, was entertained in a house may be just the right romantic touch that will close the deal.

With such an old house, the dealer generally quotes a price for it dismembered and ready to be moved to its new site. Since the cost of transportation varies with the distance, the trucking charge is customarily given as a separate item. In general, the dealer will undertake delivery at a lower figure than any one else. Also, such a dealer or an associated contractor will set a sum at which he will re-erect the structure on the new site. Since he is accustomed to working with old materials and knows just what problems he faces, his price will be lower than the combination of the cost of the old house and the price set for its rebuilding by a contractor unfamiliar with such work. The latter, to protect himself from unforeseen contingencies, must naturally add a proportionately large sum to his estimated cost.

The exact cost of an old house re-erected on a new site cannot be given off-hand. There are too many elements to be considered. How extensive are the changes, how many baths, what type of heating system, are only a few. All are important factors that must be determined before the final figure can be set. So, the prospective buyer must have patience and understanding. Also, he should have his architect prepare plans for the work with just as much thoroughness as if it were a new building. To the layman it may all seem very complicated but to an architect who knows his old houses, it is no more difficult than new work. He begins by making a careful set of measured drawings of the old house as it stands. He examines the fabric to determine what sills, beams and other parts are unsound and must be replaced. He takes as many photographs of details of the construction, both inside and out, as seem expedient and labels the prints explicitly so that they relate directly to his plans. Later, when rebuilding is under way these snap-shots will refresh his memory and make it easier to explain some special feature or unique construction to workmen who never saw the house before.

Dismembering houses for re-erection is accomplished by two methods. The more common is taking them apart board by board and timber by timber, marking each piece by a system of numbers and colors so that it can be returned to its proper place. The other is called "flaking." Here roof, side walls, and partitions are cut into large panels and numbered and marked in colors. At the new site they are put in place much as a portable bungalow is assembled.

With either method, plans prepared by the architect are of prime importance. One set of his blue prints is thoroughly annotated with numbers and colored marks. This becomes the working key, the solution to the rebuilding puzzle. Also, the plans serve as the basis for rearrangement of rooms, shifting of partitions, and the introduction of plumbing, heating, and electricity. Invariably an old house has one or more tucked-up rooms that under present-day conditions can wisely be eliminated and the space added to adjoining ones.

A favorite arrangement with old New England farmhouses was the parlor bedroom, located, as the name indicates, on the ground floor and connected by a doorway with that room of ceremony and funerals. Although it was often little larger than a double bed, it was the master bedroom of the period. Our ideas have changed and such a room can wisely be eliminated. Again, there is the problem of space for baths and closets. The former were, of course, unknown and the latter woefully few when the house was young. Thus, with the bedroom floor, architect and owner have before them a problem demanding skillful contriving to devise locations for these two essentials.

When dismembering starts, the man doing it and the building contractor, unless by a happy circumstance he is one and the same person, must work together closely. The first thing is to remove doors, window sash, and as much of the interior trim as possible, along with all the hardware. Numbered and marked, these are stored in some dry shed or barn. If feasible, they can best be left at the old site until the reconstruction has progressed far enough so that they may be put in place when delivered. All fireplaces are now examined carefully to determine the exact angles of sides and backs. The individual stones must also be numbered and keyed. Paint is applied, that will not rub off as the stones are removed.

Now everything is ready for the dramatic tearing apart. With flaking, the roof and walls are marked off in great squares related to the timber framework beneath. Then it is only a matter of sharp saws, muscle, and patience before the house has been reduced to panels, loaded on trucks, and started toward the new location.

The task is not as simple with dismembering but it, too, starts at the ridge pole and gradually works to the foundation. While one crew is clearing away the roofing, another is taking off the exterior siding. If this happens to be the original wide clapboards, great care is exercised so they may be used again. This may or may not be true of the boarding underneath. Even old builders were wont to use second-hand lumber where it wouldn't show. On the other hand, where the exterior is shingled the side walls underneath are often of wide soft wood plank which take the place of both weather boarding and supporting studs. They are, of course, numbered and removed to be used again. Shingles, whether roof or side wall, cannot be saved as they are invariably too weatherbeaten. Lath and plaster are likewise destroyed in the dismembering but they are small loss as they are usually in bad order.

If the studding is in good condition, it is used again but if it is badly warped or of oak, it is left behind. Century-old oak is as hard as concrete and must actually be drilled for nails. When the studding is taken out, all window frames and doorways are removed and stored.

Now comes removal of stairways, feather-board partitioning, flooring and paneling in the order mentioned. Offhand one would schedule the latter as one of the first things to be taken out but the building ways of the old workmen dictate otherwise. As a means of stopping drafts, they put all paneling in from joist to joist, that is, from below the upper surface of the flooring to above the lower surface of the ceiling. After floors and ceilings are out, it is a simple matter to loosen all paneling and remove it in large units. Wherever possible whole room-ends go intact. The stairway is also taken out as a unit, especially the more elaborate one in the front hall. Prying loose the old wide flooring is a difficult operation. The original hand-wrought nails have rusted fast and if too much leverage is used, the boards split. Men used to such work salvage the old flooring with little damage, however.

At the same time that the paneling makes its exit, the large hearthstones are pried from position and moved to a waiting truck. All that now remain are the chimney and timber frame. By this time each joint of the latter has been numbered and given its color code. With a simple derrick and ropes and pulleys, dismembering the frame commences. The pins that make the joints tight are removed by driving or boring. Roof rafters and purlins come first; then the yard arms that brace plate and summer beams, followed by these timbers themselves. Second floor joists come after them, followed by the corner posts. Each must be removed with caution and ingenuity. There must be no sawing apart or proper re-erection will be impossible. Since first floor rafters and sills are usually badly decayed, the general practice is to use new material. So the old ones are left behind.

While this is in progress, two men pry lintels, cheeks, and other large stones from the fireplaces, as well as stones at the openings of brick ovens. As many old bricks from the chimney are salvaged as possible. Large stone door steps are also removed but generally no attempt is made to take along the dressed stone of the foundations. The cost of hauling to the new site is out of proportion to the advantage gained. Native stones uncovered in digging the new cellar are made reasonably square and used instead. Old houses antedating 1800 are not usually over twelve or sixteen inches above the level of the ground and so little new stone is needed.

The chimney of the reconstructed house must outwardly resemble the original. Where it comes through the roof it is of ample proportions and built of old brick, but except for old fireplaces and ovens, it is otherwise modern. With flue tile, cement, mortar and hard brick, safety of construction is accomplished in much less space. What is saved frequently becomes closets or the well for plumbing pipes.

Finding space for baths is a nice game of ingenuity. Perhaps there is a small bedroom that can be divided and provide baths for two main bedrooms. Again, shifting a partition a few feet may do it. In one old house, once a tavern, the dance hall on the second floor was reduced nearly ten feet and the space became a combination bath and dressing room. Thus, the rural ball room was translated into a large master bedroom with all present-day appurtenances. In another house a storage space six by eight feet became an excellent bath by having a window cut in the exterior wall.

In the all-important question of kitchen and servants' quarters be modern from start to finish. The old farmhouse kitchen was both living room and workroom. It was large and cheerful. Accordingly the reconstructed house continues it as a living room. The new kitchen can best be located in an extension either original or new but designed to be in keeping. Here the noises and odors of cooking will not permeate the main structure and with mouse-proof new partitions, kitchen, pantry, and servants' quarters can be arranged so they will be logical and convenient. Wherever possible the garage ought to be a part of the service wing for ease of access and heating in winter.

Because of the individuality of old houses, returning doors and windows to the original location is not entirely mandatory. One here and there can be moved a little without destroying resemblance to the original. With the plans for re-erection complete, everything is ready for a second raising of the frame. New sills cut to the same dimensions as the old are put in place. Then corner posts, summer and plate beams, and other principal timbers are hoisted to their proper places. By virtue of numbering and marking with colors—red for the ground floor, blue for the second, and black for the attic is one reconstructor's code—each mortice and tenon joint is put back just as it was originally and the whole frame made plumb. Now hardwood pins driven home at its joints make the skeleton firm and solid. Then comes the new roof of whatever type of shingles selected. Along with it starts the work of enclosing the side walls. These steps, of course, apply to a structure taken apart piecemeal. With a "flaked" house, roofs and walls are returned to position as panels. Making saw-cut cracks tight is the only remaining step.

If possible, the old studding and weather boarding are used, although, as neither will show, new material can be substituted if desired. Similarly a rough flooring of cheap lumber is laid as a foundation for the old. Such features as the main stairway and paneling, cleaned and repaired, are now brought in through large openings in the side walls and put in place before enclosing the frame is completed.

There are two points of view about using old window frames. One favors using them despite lack of mechanical means for raising or lowering the sash. The other, reasoning that many of the frames are bound to be badly weathered and not too sound, recommends new ones complete with weights and cords. With the latter, the old effect is preserved by reproducing the exterior molding exactly and by using the original interior trim.

After enclosing is completed and the interior partitions are in place, the house is ready for lath and plaster. Wood or metal lath or any one of the various plaster boards can be used as foundation. Now comes a fine point. Present-day plasterers produce a much finer finish than was the rule a century ago, but if they understand the effect desired they will restrain themselves and possibly omit the final skim coat.

The next details are the window sash, interior trim, and the final exterior siding. The latter can be either the original clapboards, new ones of the same width, or the long riven shingles. Whatever is used, for protection against winter winds, the boarding ought to be sheathed either with building paper or a quilting. Likewise, the tops of all door and window frames must be properly flashed. This prevents rain leaks which are bound to stain the plaster.

Before the original flooring is re-laid it should be thoroughly scrubbed with a mild lye solution to rid it of old paint, stains, and dirt; as many of the old nails removed as possible, and injured sections discarded. Since there is bound to be an appreciable loss, the attic flooring can be used to take the place of that discarded or an additional amount bought from some wrecker specializing in materials salvaged from old structures. Along with cleaning the old flooring, it is frequently wise to have the edges re-planed so they will be straight and true. It obviates wide cracks that gather dust and lint.

**AS THEY BUILT A CHIMNEY IN THE EIGHTEENTH CENTURY**

*Photo by John Runyon*

In taking the old house apart, a bit of siding may give a clue to the original color outside. Under the various coats of paint and paper of the interior the owner may get glimpses of the scheme of decoration used when the house was young. We may not realize it but Colonial Americans were partial to color in the home and used a number of very effective off-shades now largely forgotten. If these can be discovered and samples preserved for matching, the results will be authentic and at the same time give the house an individuality and atmosphere that will not be met with elsewhere.

A house that can be purchased for removal will not often be completely equipped with its original wrought-iron hinges, door latches and locks. But the chances are that enough will remain to indicate what they were and replacements that match and fit can be bought from an antique dealer specializing in old hardware.

Since electricity is entirely a modern convenience, selecting fixtures must depend entirely on the owner's taste. One of the most satisfactory restored houses we have seen has very few fixtures and many portable lamps chiefly made from old jugs and converted astral oil lamps. In bathrooms, kitchen, cellar and garage, no attempt was made to affect the antique. Being strictly utilitarian rooms, simple fixtures that would provide the maximum of light were employed.

So "if only" has become an actuality. The old house is now comfortably settled on its new site and like most transplanted things will thrive better if some faint flavor of its old surroundings is present, such as an apple orchard or one or two fine old trees that look as if they and the house had grown old together.

# CHAPTER VIII

## THE SMOKE GOES UP THE CHIMNEY

"Remember that the new chimneys are not to smoke," wrote General Washington from New York in 1776 to his kinsman and overseer, Lund Washington, regarding the remodeling of Mount Vernon. That admonition is just as necessary today as then. A chimney is still an essential part of a house. Also, despite the newest and most effective heating systems, family life, in the country at least, still centers around the hearth. Old, new, or merely middle-aged, no country home is considered properly equipped without at least one fireplace.

There is no use in pretending that they are needed for heat, but the leaping flames and brisk crackling of burning twigs are a cheery sight and sound. "Harriet *will* have her fireplace fire even though she has to open all the doors and windows," chuckled one householder. This ceases to be a pleasantry if doors and windows have to be thrown wide to let out smoke instead of excess heat. Then this center of family cheer becomes as exasperating as any other inanimate thing that doesn't work.

If, by purchase of an existing structure, a householder has become heir to such a problem, simple things, like fireplace hoods, capping the chimney, or increasing its height, can be tried. If these fail, architectural counsel is the next step. Such trouble is more frequent in houses dating after the stove era than before. The old masons built fireplaces for practical use rather than for occasional indulgence.

They had never heard of aerodynamics but they knew how to construct fireplaces that would give out real heat as well as chimneys that carried the smoke where it belonged, up and out.

Of course some unwise features are to be found in the old work but, for the most part, design and proportions cannot be improved. The angles of sides and back, size of opening and throat, location of smoke shelf, size and proportions of smoke chamber, all were determined through years of rule of thumb experiment where only the best results survived. Therefore, the owner of an antique country home with chimney and fireplaces intact should think twice before he gives orders to demolish them. Similarly, he who is building a new house can well plan to reproduce the old fireplaces in size and shape.

Building proper chimneys and hearths was slowly evolved through the centuries. In the late 18th century, an American codified this masonic lore and established the scientific basis for a proper fireplace so cogently that even today his principles form the backbone of fireplace building. He was born Benjamin Thompson, March 26, 1753, at Woburn, Massachusetts, but is better known as Count von Rumford of the Holy Roman Empire.

"The plague of a smoking fireplace is proverbial," began Rumford in his treatise on the subject, written during his years in the service of the Elector of Bavaria. Stripped of the involved terminology characteristic of the natural philosopher of that day, his specifications for a smokeless, heat-radiating fireplace are very simple and depend on three fundamentals. First, the size of flue must be in proportion to the fireplace opening. Second, the angles of back and jambs must be such that they will reflect heat into the room. Third, throat and smoke chamber of proper size and shape are essential because the former improves the draft while the latter prevents smoke from being blown out into the room by a down draft within the chimney flue.

From this it is clear that the New England-reared count of the Holy Roman Empire was really describing the type and design of fireplace in general use at home in his boyhood and explaining the scientific reasons for its superiority over European rectangular ones, built throatless and without a smoke chamber. As stated before, technical men today generally go back to Rumford's work and the American tradition behind it, but in one particular they make a wise departure. Instead of a single common flue, they advocate separate ones for each fireplace.

These modern specifications, based on several centuries of good practice, are as follows: The fireplace should be at least 18 inches deep and have a hearth 20 inches wide. The size of opening must of course be in proportion to the dimensions of the room, but one with lintel less that 26 inches above the hearth is not practical because of difficulty in tending the fire. A good maximum height is 42 inches. The width should be in accord and exceed it so that the opening is a well-proportioned rectangle with its greater dimension horizontal.

In our country home, built about 1765, there are three fireplaces, each of different size and proportions. The largest, where the cooking was done, is 50 inches wide by 37 inches high and 18 inches deep. The one in the old parlor has a width of

38-1/2 inches, a height of 28-1/2 inches, and a depth of 13-1/2 inches. The smallest has an opening just off the square which is 27 inches wide by 25-1/2 inches high with a depth of only 11 inches. All three are non-smokers under all conditions of wind and weather. With proper size of wood they are easy to tend and good sources of warmth except in real winter weather. Each is individualistic in hearth dimensions, the largest of course being that of the old kitchen with a hearthstone over seven feet long by two feet wide.

Whether heat radiates into the room, or goes up the chimney along with the smoke, depends on the angles of fireplace sides and back. The former should be set at an angle of about 60 degrees so that they flare outward from the back wall. There are two schools of thought regarding the back. One would have the forward pitch begin one third of the distance from floor to lintel; the other favors the slope starting at the bottom and continuing upward in an unbroken plane. In the former, the pitch should be about 23 degrees from the vertical; with the latter, 18 degrees will suffice.

From this point the consideration of dimensions goes up the chimney. In its standard ordinance for chimney construction, the National Board of Fire Underwriters calls for fireplace flues with a draft area of one-twelfth of that of the fireplace opening and determines this area as a circle or ellipse that will fit within the tile used to line the flue. As it is difficult to obtain flue linings of exactly the desired area, it is better to select a size slightly larger, rather than one smaller, and so make sure of sufficient capacity under all weather conditions.

Between the lintel of the fireplace and the point where the flue commences come the three structural features so stressed by Count Rumford. They are the throat, smoke shelf, and smoke chamber. As its name implies, the throat is the opening through which smoke, hot gases, and some flames pass on their way upward. Experts hold that its correct construction contributes more to the efficiency of a fireplace than any other feature, save proper flue design. The area of the throat opening should not be less than that of the flue and its length must be equal to the width of the fireplace. It should be located eight inches above the lintel. Under present practice, a cast-iron throat with a damper which can be opened and closed to regulate the up-chimney flow is standard. Also, when the fireplace is not in use, this damper can be closed and so prevent loss of other heat.

The smoke shelf comes immediately above the throat and is formed by recessing the brickwork of the back the full width of the chimney for at least four inches. With very large fireplaces, it may be as much as twelve inches. The object of this feature is to stop any accidental draft within the flue from going farther and blowing smoke out into the room. The area in between this and the flue itself is called the smoke chamber. Here the walls are drawn in with a gradual upward taper to the point where the flue lining begins. The chamber so formed can and does hold accumulated smoke temporarily when a gust of wind across the chimney top cuts off the draft for a moment.

In building chimneys, the old masons varied their structural ways and materials according to the part of the country in which they worked. New England workmen were partial to a central chimney, the core around which the house was built, and their usual material was stone. Occasionally brick was used but this material was more in favor with old houses of the middle states and the South. Here, instead of the central stack, a chimney was built in each of the two end walls. The climate was milder and the style of architecture, with central hall and stairway, made such practice desirable.

The mark of an old chimney is its massive construction. In those of the central type, it is not uncommon to find a foundation pier of ten by twelve feet in the cellar. This was laid dry and just below the level of the first floor, large transverse beams were put in place to support the hearthstones of the fireplaces above. Here dry work stopped and, from there to the chimney top, all stones were laid in a mortar made of lime and sand. At a point above the smoke chambers of the various fireplaces and the brick-oven flue (always a part of the kitchen fireplace) all came together in a common flue. Here the chimney gradually tapered to the top and was usually about three or four feet square where it came through the roof. Originally such chimneys were entirely of stone. Comparatively few are found in original condition today. Time and weather usually made repair or repointing of the portion above the roof line necessary and, in the course of it, brick was often used instead of stone.

By ample proportions the old masons achieved fire safety. This can now be accomplished with a distinct saving in space if one is building a new chimney. There are certain fundamental provisions as stated in the standard chimney ordinance cited above. These are tedious and complicated reading for the layman, but to architects, builders and masons, they simply mean standard workmanship and materials that have been used for years to insure correctly functioning chimneys. Possibly a brief resumé of these fundamentals is not out of place in order that the prospective country house owner may not demand the impossible in his schemes for convenient closets, cupboards, or even a stairway.

The chimney may be built of brick, stone, reinforced concrete, concrete blocks, or hollow tile of clay or concrete.

All chimneys should rest on an adequate foundation located below the frost line and both chimney and flues should adhere strictly to the perpendicular.

If an angle is necessary, it ought not to be greater than 45 degrees.

No offset should be over three-eighths of the total width of the chimney.

In laying brick or other material, care should be taken that all joints are tight and completely filled with mortar.

Unlined chimneys are not prohibited but the best arrangement is one in which all flues are lined with fire clay tile, joints well set in mortar, and each flue separated by a partition of brick. Only sound, uncracked tile should be put in place.

Fireplace walls must be of ample proportions to support the chimney and at least eight inches thick. It is further suggested that they be lined with fire brick.

The woodwork around fireplaces must not be closer than four inches to the back wall of a chimney and floor beams must be two inches away from a chimney wall. The space between should be filled with loose crushed cinders or other porous incombustible material to form a fire stop.

Plaster for exterior walls of a chimney should be applied direct or on metal lath. No wood furring or lath.

The hearth, which may be of brick, stone, tile, or concrete, must be supported by a masonry trimmer arch or similar fire-resisting construction. Both hearth and arch should be at least twenty inches wide and not less than two feet longer than the width of the fireplace opening.

If the mantel is of wood, it must not be placed within eight inches of the jambs, or twelve of the lintel.

The minimum height of chimneys above the roof line is two feet for hip, gable, or mansard roofs, and three for flat ones.

Chimney caps must not reduce the effective draft area of flues.

In connecting the smoke pipe of a heating plant, incinerator, or water heater to its flue in the chimney, the opening must be built with a fire clay tile collar and the smoke pipe should not protrude into the flue beyond the collar. Otherwise, the efficiency of the draft is materially impaired.

In addition, home owners may have other features installed that will do much to increase heat production of fireplaces and convenience in the use of them. One is the steel fireplace form, built into the chimney. This takes the place of jambs, back, throat, smoke shelf, and smoke chamber and is so designed that behind sides and back there is an air space opening into the room through intake and outlet vents on either side of the fireplace. The cold air of the room is drawn into this space, heated by radiation and returned. It acts on the order of a hot air furnace and can be used to advantage in new fireplaces or in old ones too much out of repair to be used without rebuilding.

There is also the sheet-steel smoke chamber which comes complete with throat damper and smoke shelf and is put in place above the lintel where it extends to the point where the flue commences. A common device for easy disposal of the ashes is the ash dump, a small cast-iron vault located in the fireplace floor and connected with an ash vault built in the chimney foundation. The vault is equipped with an iron door so that the ashes may be removed once or twice a year.

So much for chimneys and fireplaces. For actual and even heating of all parts of the house, some type of heating plant is necessary both for comfort and economy. It is true that our forefathers lived, many of them to a ripe old age, with only fireplaces to heat their drafty homes and with no heat at all in their public buildings. They did, however, fortify themselves well with a daily draft of rum and they wore a quantity of clothing that would be intolerable today. Further, plenty of wood for fuel grew at their very door; it was part of the normal farm work to cut it down and prepare it for the cavernous fireplaces.

But then, as now, a fireplace could only heat a comparatively small area. Further, under modern conditions, it is the most expensive heat that can be generated. Even though your holding includes a good sized wood-lot, the cost of labor for getting fuel cut, drawn, and piled in your cellar may run to more than the same amount purchased from the local coal yard.

If you have purchased an old house with no heating plant or are building a new house, the type of heating used will largely depend on what your architect considers practical and what you can pay for. The chief systems, viewed in descending order of expense, are hot water, steam, piped hot air, and the pipeless furnace. All of these can be fitted to burn either coal or oil.

Provided one can meet the initial expense of purchase and installation, the ideal system is probably the oil burning, electrically run, hot water heating system. Barring the final perfection of the robot, it is as near to a mechanical servant as one is likely to get even in this age of invention. There is no shoveling or sifting of ashes. There is no furnace shaking or stoking, no puzzling over dampers. Periodically and for a price, a man comes and fills the oil tank. A thermostat regulates the heat. You have only to set it for the desired temperature and forget it.

There is just one flaw with this perfect system. It is dependent on electricity. Let that fail and there is trouble. The fine copper radiators, so efficient when all goes well, spring leaks if the water in them freezes. A few years ago an unusually severe blizzard in the North Atlantic states worked havoc with all of the modern devices. Roads were blocked, telephone and electric service lines were down, and even train service was impaired. One of our neighbors had built a new house two or three years before and equipped it with practically every appliance known to modern comfort, including an oil burner.

In a few short hours this blizzard had set him back more than a century. Electricity, of course, failed and the heat in his fine furnace dwindled and died. It grew colder and colder, ultimately reaching twenty degrees below zero. Added to the discomfort of the family was the disquieting knowledge that the freezing point would mean cracked radiators. Luckily he had three fireplaces that really worked. He had plenty of wood. So for three days and nights, he and two other members of his family worked in relays to keep roaring fires going in all three fireplaces. In this way they maintained a temperature of at least 40 degrees and so saved pipes and radiators.

One may argue that, if water freezing in radiators and pipes is all, why not drain them in such an emergency. This is a job for a plumber, as it must be done with a thoroughness that leaves no moisture behind. The average layman has neither the skill nor the tools for it. Therefore, if there comes a winter when snow, ice, high winds, and low temperatures cause you to wonder if living in the country the year around is quite sound and you decide that a few weeks in a nice city apartment would be a good idea, close your house, if it seems more expedient than leaving a caretaker behind, but don't try to save the plumber's fee. Remember pipes, radiators, and valves cannot be mended. They have to be replaced and that is expensive.

However, blizzards that seriously interrupt electric service are so rare that one need not forego the decided comfort that an oil burner gives, just because some such chance may arise. Also, if the question of expense must be considered, steam can be used instead of hot water and will cost from one-quarter to one-third less.

The initial expenditure for both hot water and steam heating is considerably less, too, if coal rather than oil is to be the fuel. This calls for quite a little more supervision on the part of the householder. He can cut down some of the drudgery of stoking by installing a gravity feed type of boiler. This is equipped with a hopper and needs filling only once a day. Or he can use the old fashioned hand-fired type, with or without the services of a man of all work. There will be dust and dirt as well as the morning and evening rituals of stoking, adjusting dampers, shaking, and cleaning out the ash pit. There will be the periodic chore of sifting ashes and carrying them out for either carting away or for filling in hollow places in the driveway. But his fire will burn, no matter what happens to the current of the local light and power company.

However, as already stated, electricity is a faithful servant most of the time and there are devices that not only take away some of the drudgery of furnace tending but, in the long run, actually save money in coal bills. One of these is the mechanical stoker which is electrically driven and burns the finest size of coal. Another way of reducing the coal bill is to install an electric blower. This, as its name implies, is a forced draft controlled by a thermostat, and with it the cheaper grades of coal can be used. Incidentally, any coal-burning furnace that gets to sulking can be made to respond by placing an ordinary electric fan before the open ash pit. We have done this with a pipeless furnace and have been able to burn the cheaper buckwheat coal almost entirely as a result.

There appears to be no mechanical device for removing the ashes out of the cellar. So, if the householder puts in a coal burning steam or hot water plant as a matter of economy, and then in a few years covets an oil burner, it is perfectly practical and possible to have one installed in his furnace. Whatever the fuel, make sure enough radiation is provided with steam or hot water plants to heat the house evenly and adequately in the coldest weather according to your ideas rather than the plumber's. He is usually a hardy individual who considers 68 degrees warm enough for any one. Theoretically it may be. Actually most people are more comfortable at a room temperature of from two to four degrees higher.

Cheapest of all to install and operate is the pipeless furnace. This is hardly more than a large stove set in the cellar. An ample register in the floor directly above it is connected to a galvanized iron casing that surrounds the fire pot. It is divided so that cool air from the house itself is drawn downward, heated, and then forced upward again. This system will not work well in a house equipped with wings or additions so placed that the air from the central register cannot penetrate. It is particularly effective in a house with a central hall.

In the 18th century compact house with central chimney, the pipeless furnace register can be set in the small front entrance and another register cut in the ceiling directly above it. This carries part of the heat to the second floor and so makes for better distribution of the warm air. As already stated, such a furnace is quite inexpensive and so easy to install that the average handy man will not find it too complicated. We put one in our country home some eight years ago merely as a means of keeping the house warm during the early spring and late fall. We have since found that it can and does heat the entire house even at sub-zero temperatures.

In all honesty, however, one must admit that it has certain disadvantages. First, it is like the old-fashioned stove in that an even heat is hard to maintain. Second, with coal or wood as the usual fuel, there is a discouraging amount of dust generated. Third, the doors to all rooms must be left open so that the currents of hot air can circulate. One chooses between frosty seclusion and balmy gregariousness. Yet, in spite of these very definite "outs," it is far better than no furnace at all. It is, in fact, an excellent stop gap for the country house owner who is not prepared to invest in the more expensive heating plants at the moment. The more effete system can always be added later and the faithful old pipeless junked, moved to some other building, or left in place for an emergency, such as a public-utility-crippling blizzard or flood.

# CHAPTER IX

## THE QUESTION OF WATER SUPPLY

Whether one lives in the country or the city, geology and geography govern the source of the water that flows from the tap. Cities go miles for an adequate, pure water supply and have been doing so since the days of the Caesars. Such systems involve thousands of acres and millions of dollars for water sheds, reservoirs, dams, pipe lines, and purifying plants.

The country place is a miniature municipality with its own water system. The latter need not be elaborate or expensive but it must be adequate. Nothing disrupts a family so quickly and completely as water shortage. Personally, we would far rather see our family hungry and in rags than again curtail its baths and showers. "We can be careful and only use what is necessary," sounds easy but before long everybody is against father. He is mean and unreasonable. Save the water, indeed! It is all his fault. He should have known the supply would fail when he bought the place. A moron could see it was not large enough. A six weeks' drought? Well, what of it!

Meanwhile water diviners, well diggers and drillers add gall and wormwood to the situation. "Oh yes, that well always did go dry about this time of year, Saving the water wouldn't make any difference. Better not bother with it but dig or drill a new one." Expense? Why quibble about that when the peace of one's family is at stake. There is, of course, only one outcome. A broken and chastened man soon makes the best terms he can with one of his tormentors. If he is wise it will be with the advocate of the driven well. That solves for all time any question of water supply.

Before deciding on a source, however, consider what the daily needs will be. From long observation, it has been found that the average country place requires fifty gallons of water a day for each member of the family, servants included. Then allow for two extra people so that the occasional guest, whose knowledge of water systems begins and ends with the turning of a faucet, will not unduly deplete the supply. For example, a family of seven should have a daily water supply of from 400 to 500 gallons depending on how much entertaining is done and how extensive are the outdoor uses. This allowance will be ample for toilets, baths, kitchen and laundry, as well as for moderate watering of the garden and lawn. Of course, if cars are to be washed regularly, fifty gallons should be added to the daily demand. If there is a swimming pool, its capacity should be figured by cubical content multiplied by seven and one-half (the number of gallons to the cubic foot) and allowance made for from fifteen to twenty-five per cent fresh water daily.

The daily production of a spring or drilled well can be easily gauged. A flow of one gallon a minute produces 1,440 gallons in twenty-four hours. In other words, a flow of ten gallons a minute means 14,400 gallons a day which, at fifteen gallons a bath or shower, is enough water to wash a regiment from the colonel to the newest recruit.

Estimating the daily production of a shallow, dug well is more difficult. The number of gallons standing in it can be obtained by using the mathematical formula for the contents of a cylinder, but only observation will tell how quickly the well replenishes itself when pumped dry. By long experience, however, country plumbers have found that if such a well contains five feet of water in extremely dry weather, it can be relied upon for the needed fifty gallons a day each for a family of seven with enough over for safety.

In fact, with all water sources except an artesian or driven well, the question always is, will it last during an abnormally rainless season? Never-failing springs and wells that never go dry are institutions in any countryside. So consult some of the oldest inhabitants. They know and if they give your well or spring a good character, the chances are that even the most exacting of families will find such a water supply adequate. Whether it is pure or not is another matter but one that can easily be determined by sending a sample to your state health department or a bacteriological laboratory. That this should be done before such water is used for drinking purposes goes without saying.

The driven or artesian well has two points that makes it worth the cost. There is no question of purity or of quantity. It taps subterranean water which is unaffected by local causes of contamination or by drought.

The kind of water system, like the supply, is governed by geography and geology. If there happens to be a spring on a nearby hillside somewhat higher than the house, nature has provided the cheapest and simplest system. A pipe line and storage tank are all that are needed. Gravity does the rest. On the other hand, if the spring is on the same level or lower than the house, a pump must be added to the equipment to force the water into the pressure tank and out of the faucets. If the spring has a large flow and adequate drainage, a water ram is advisable. With this hydraulic machine, three-quarters of the water that flows into it is used to force the balance into the storage tank. The expense of operation is nothing and as water rams and pumps cost about the same, such an installation has much to recommend it.

When the search for water goes below ground, one must reckon with geology. What lies below the turf is the deciding factor. If it is sand and gravel with a high water table (the level of subterranean water), an excellent well can be had cheaply. The practice is either to bore through to the water table with a man-operated auger and then insert the pipe, or to drive the latter down with a heavy sledge hammer. In either case, water is but a few feet below ground and a shallow-well pump, which can raise water twenty-two feet by suction, will be adequate.

There are two types of well to be considered with less favorable subsoil formations — the shallow and the artesian. With the former (known to country people as a dug well) a shaft from six to ten feet across is dug with pick and shovel until adequate water is reached. Then the shaft is lined with stone laid without cement or mortar up to a few feet from the top. This allows water from the surrounding area to seep into the well where it is retained until it is drawn upward by the pump. It is obvious that a well of this type cannot be built through ledge or solid rock. In fact, unusually large boulders sometimes force diggers to abandon a shaft and start afresh. An old house with two or three of these shallow wells on the premises serves notice on the prospective buyer that repeated and probably unsuccessful attempts have been made to find a well that does not go dry.

Dug wells are seldom deeper than fifty feet; the majority are but little beyond twenty-two feet, the suction limit for a shallow-well pump. As is obvious from their construction, they depend on the water in the upper layers of the subsoil and so are more readily affected by dry weather. Although not drought-proof like the artesian, a dug well, which costs much less, can be an excellent water source and supply amazingly large quantities of water.

We have lived for ten years in a house served by a shallow well credited with being never failing and it has faithfully lived up to its reputation, even through the driest of seasons. Once, however, it made real trouble. Over it stood a picturesque latticed well house. On one of the beams a pair of robins nested annually. In the middle of the third summer the water developed a queer flavor. It steadily grew stronger until one night the steam arising from a hot bath caused the pajama-clad head of the house to seize a flashlight and move hastily to the well house. One beam of light disclosed the horrid truth. Floating in the water far below were two very dead fledglings.

The next day a well cleaner collected twenty-five dollars for removing the birds and pumping out the well. He also gave some excellent advice which was followed promptly. The well house, picturesque though it was, gave way to a substantial masonry curbing equipped with a stout wire cover. The peace of mind so gained has more than offset the trifling expense. No longer need one peer fearfully down a twenty-five foot shaft when a pet cat fails to show up for a meal, or shoo away from the spot the over-inquisitive offspring of visiting friends.

The drilled well, against which there is no possible argument save that of cost, is made by boring a hole in the ground with a powerful apparatus until sufficient subterranean water is reached. There are two methods, the chop and the core drill. With the former, a cutting tool exactly like the drill used to drive holes in rocks for blasting, only larger, cuts a circular hole downward. The boom of the drilling rig as it raises and drops the drill provides the necessary impact. With the core method, as its name implies, a hollow boring drill cuts its way aided by steel shot and a flow of water forced through the pipe that rotates the cutting tool.

With either method the results are the same. Sooner or later the drill will reach an underground water course of sufficient size to give an ample flow. As such drilling is done on a charge of three to five dollars a foot, the owner, of course, hopes for sooner. Except where there is an underlying stratum of sand or gravel beneath hard pan, the drill has to go through rock. How far depends on the kind. Sandstone is the best water producer; limestone yields very hard water. Again, drilling through till (a heterogeneous mixture of clay, gravel, and boulders) may or may not locate water readily depending on how densely it is packed. The rocks known as gneiss and schist are readily bored and are considered fair water bearers.

Granite is bad news. It means slow work and a deep and expensive well. It is one of the hardest rocks with little water content. The only hope is that the drill will strike a vein flowing through a fissure. Whether it will be at fifty or 500 feet is a pure matter of luck. A dry well at 100 feet may become a gusher at 105 delivering twenty gallons to the minute, or it may stay dry for another two to five hundred feet.

Tales of well drilling are many and varied. Good pure water has been found at fifteen feet. In New Hampshire there is a well 900 feet deep that gushes so powerfully that it is capped and still flows at forty pounds pressure. It supplies an elaborate country place and a large stock farm. It is performances like these that indicate the water is there if one will just keep on drilling and paying until it is reached.

Where to locate a well is very much a matter of guess. Even in the Sahara Desert there is water. How far down is the question. For generations much faith was placed in diviners. They were supposedly endowed with some occult talent that enabled them to pick a sure spot for water. They were known for miles around and were summoned when a new homestead was under consideration. With a forked hazel wand held in both hands, such an one would pace solemnly around until the stick gave a convulsive twist downward. This indicated that water was directly beneath. The spot would be reverently marked; the diviner would depart and the well diggers who had followed his performance with proper awe would begin work. As the ceremony failed to stipulate just how far down the precious liquid was, a successful well was presumably the result. The prowess of the well diviner is acclaimed even today by some people, although scientific investigation has proved that his services are worth just about as much as those of a witch doctor.

After the country home owner has attended to the little matter of a well, be it old or new, dug or drilled, the next step is installing a pump. If the water level is less than twenty feet below ground, a shallow-well pump will be perfectly adequate and as it is much less expensive than the more elaborate deep-well pump, we recommend its use if possible. Most plumbers invariably advise the deep-well pump, especially for driven wells. They do this in all honesty and with no ulterior motive. There is always a bare chance that the water level may drop below the suction limit of the shallow pump under abnormal pressure. If it does, an irate customer can descend on the luckless installer of the less expensive pump and cause general unpleasantness if not loss of custom.

The difference between these two kinds of pump, aside from price, is that with a shallow-well one, suction is produced in the cylinder of the pump itself, while the deep-well pump has its plunger and cylinder at the bottom of the well. Water is forced up the pipe by the up and down movement of the plunger within the cylinder. This plunger is connected to a geared wheel by the well-rod that extends downward from well-head to cylinder in the center of the same pipe through which the water is forced upward. Because of its design, a deep-well pump must always be located directly above the well itself. With a suction pump, on the other hand, the pipe from well to pump may bend and turn to suit conditions. These should be as few as possible since each right-angle bend of the pipe reduces the pump's suction power one foot.

As for motive power, electricity has distinct advantages over all other means. The switch operated by pressure starts the pump when the supply of water in the storage tank drops below a certain level, and also stops it when the proper volume has been reached. (Ten pounds to start the pump and forty or fifty to stop it are the usual adjustments.) A nice little refinement here is the installation of a third faucet at either kitchen or pantry sink, piped direct to the pump. Turn this and fresh water flows from the well itself, thus consoling any sentimentalist with visions of a dripping moss-covered bucket. Also water so drawn seldom needs to be iced. In summer if there are signs of a thunder storm it is wise to open this same faucet. It starts the pump and that automatically continues until the storage tank is full. Then, if electric service is cut off by the storm, the household will have ample water until the damage has been repaired.

If the country home owner happens to live beyond reach of an electric light system, he can put in his own plant, use a gasoline engine for motive power or even a hand pump. A gasoline engine should, of course, be located in an outbuilding and the exhaust pipe must extend into open air because of the deadly fumes of carbon monoxide gas. The hand pump is, of course, the simplest and there are several excellent ones to be had. They are not as practical as they sound, however.

## A PLACE FOR SUMMER AND WEEK-ENDS

*Robertson Ward, architect. Photo by La Roche*

When we first bought our own country place we installed a very good one as there was then no electricity in the locality. It worked excellently—when any one could be found to man it. Handy men hired for odd jobs around the grounds took it on for a set sum per time. The labor turnover was unprecedented. One by one they either resigned within a week or somehow managed to "forget all about that pumping job." Members of the family pressed into service straightway became ardent water savers, and guests who volunteered gallantly somehow never, never came again. Yet it was not an exhausting or complicated task. It was simply so monotonous that it wore down the most phlegmatic nature. So the rural householder will do well to remember that, after all, this is a machine age and govern himself accordingly.

As for the storage tank, the modern practice is to place it under ground or in the cellar. The old custom of putting it in the attic had distinct disadvantages when an overflow or a leak occurred and either stained the ceilings or sent them crashing down on furniture and possibly occupants of the rooms below.

The best water system, however, cannot cope with faucets thoughtlessly left running. Even the largest tank will eventually become empty and then there will be water for no one until the pump has replenished the supply. "Waste not, want not" is an excellent motto for dwellers in the country, especially where water is concerned.

# CHAPTER X

## SEWAGE SAFETY

Among the problems which his miniature municipality brings to the country house owner is the unromantic but necessary one of sewage disposal. In a suburban area it is merely a matter of connecting the house to the street main and paying higher taxes. With the country house, each owner must cope with the question for himself. He cannot leave it to chance or delude himself that any old system will serve. Some hot August day when his house is filled with guests, the makeshift disposal system will suddenly cease to function and an otherwise tactful guest will ask whether that queer smell is just part of the regular country air or what.

Of course, nobody thinks of disposing of household waste by piping it to a brook or letting it flow down a sandy side hill some distance from the house. Those were the methods of the ignorant and unscientific past. The means of disposal recommended by sanitary experts are those in which the wastes undergo a bacterial fermentation which finally renders the sewage odorless and harmless. It can be accomplished by a septic tank or a tight cesspool. The latter with its two chambers is really a variety of the septic tank itself. The first vault is built of stone or brick laid in mortar and covered with a coat of waterproof cement. With both supply and overflow pipes below the normal level of the liquids, beneficial fermentation takes place in this compartment before the liquids pass over into the second chamber from which they gradually seep into the ground. Such an installation calls for more excavation and construction than a septic tank and, since it accomplishes nothing that cannot be done with the latter, is only used where there is not enough ground area for the disposal fields of a septic tank.

The latter is an air-tight cylindrical or oblong container placed below ground, in which raw sewage purifies itself by the inherent bacteria. The first stage takes place within the tank and the second in the porous pipes that constitute the disposal fields. From the moment household wastes enter the tank, fermentation begins its work of reducing them from noisome sewage to harmless water. Both intake and outlet pipes extend below the level of the contents, with a baffle plate across the center which prevents direct outward flow. The heavy solids sink to the bottom and anaerobic bacteria, which develop only where there is no oxygen, breed rapidly and break these up so that they rise to the top and provide the ever present scum which excludes all air and stimulates fermentation of the entire content. Meanwhile, liquid from the tank is flowing into the disposal fields, which are porous land tile laid in shallow trenches and covered with earth and sod. Here some air is present and aerobic bacteria (those which thrive where there is oxygen) develop and complete the process of transforming the wastes into clear water.

Installing such a system is neither expensive nor complicated. The tank itself should be large enough to hold the sewage of a household for twenty-four hours. It can be bought ready to install, or built of brick or concrete. Ready-made tanks are to be had of steel, concrete, or vitrified tile. We installed one of steel (which is the cheapest) some ten years ago and have found it most satisfactory. When it was delivered, two husky truck-men placed it at the edge of the pit prepared for it by the waiting plumber. They exhibited some curiosity and the plumber explained briefly about the bacteria and its action.

"You mean one of these here bugs is into it already?" asked one of them as he applied an awe-struck eye to the aperture in the top. He apparently expected to find an insect akin to a full-size cockroach running around inside, and either decided the light was poor or that the plumber was a first-class liar, for he went off shaking his head doubtfully.

The size of tank and length of disposal field is entirely a matter of size of household. On an average, the daily volume can be reckoned on the basis of fifty gallons per person and, for every fifty gallons of tank capacity, there should be thirty feet of disposal field. Thus, for a family of eight, a tank of five hundred gallons' capacity connected with a disposal field of three hundred feet will be ample, allowing for guests as well.

In installing this system, the tank itself can be as near the house as ten or fifteen feet but the piping connecting it with the soil line of the plumbing should be water tight. The best way is to use four-inch cast iron pipe, calking all joints with oakum and lead. At a convenient point between house and tank, this line of pipe should have a "clean-out" fitting so that rags, solidified grease, or other substances that might block it can be removed. Sometimes vitrified tile with cemented joints is used instead of cast-iron pipe; but it has the distinct disadvantage that, if the rootlets of trees or large shrubs, attracted by the water, find so much as a pin hole in the cement, they will grow through and finally clog the pipe.

From the tank to the disposal field, the first three or four lengths of pipe should be glazed tile with tight cement joints. From these on, three or four inch porous land tile laid in shallow trenches is used. For proper action, the trenches of the field should be not over eighteen inches deep so that the warmth and evaporation of the sun may be effective. Also in digging these trenches, there should be a slight grade away from the outlet of the tank. An inch to every ten feet is adequate.

The bottom of the trenches is covered with a two-inch layer of medium-sized crushed stone or clean gravel. On this rest the land tile, and the joints are covered with roofing paper to prevent bits of stone or gravel from lodging within the pipe. The latter is covered two inches deep with more stone or gravel and over all go lengths of roofing paper cut slightly wider than the trench so that, when in place, the paper arches and fits tightly to the sides. The purpose of the stone or gravel is to facilitate water seepage from tile to ground while the roofing paper cover prevents silt from reducing the seepage.

At the terminus of each trench is a leaching pool, built by digging a hole about three feet across and five feet deep. It is filled with crushed stone or small rocks to the level of the trench piping. Over it, before replacing the dirt, goes another piece of roofing paper. Into these pools drain what water has not seeped away in flowing from the tank.

As can be seen from the foregoing description, the fermentation and bacterial action that takes place in a properly built septic tank system is automatic and needs no attention, although every second or third year it is advisable to remove the mud-like sediment from the tank. Otherwise, the latter's capacity gradually diminishes.

The steps involved in building such a system are so simple that, while the services of a plumber are advisable, it is possible for an intelligent handy man to do the work. Be sure, however, that he realizes that each step is important and necessary. We knew of one otherwise capable workman who calmly omitted the crushed stone and gravel in the tile trenches. The system worked well for about four years. Then, one warm and sticky day in July, it ceased to function. A plumber demonstrated that the tiles were clogged with silt because the bed of crushed stone had been forgotten. For a week the house was sewerless while the careless short cut was remedied. The household had but two alternatives, take a vacation or go primitive.

However, if a properly installed system fails to work, the cause lies in what it has to digest. Too much grease or too strong antiseptic solutions will reduce or prevent proper fermentation. Waste grease should therefore go into the garbage can. Also, strong doses of germ-killing solutions poured daily down sink-drains and toilets can put the hardiest septic tank out of action. The remedy for such misguided sanitary efforts is simple. Turn on all the faucets in the house and so flush the tank thoroughly. Then pour down a toilet one or two pails of warm water in which a dozen cakes of yeast have been thoroughly dissolved. The bacteria of the yeast will re-establish fermentation in the tank and all will be well if no further doses of disinfectants come along to interfere.

When one stops to consider, the septic tank is a remarkably simple and effective means of being rid of household wastes odorlessly and without contamination. Of course, such a system should be placed as far as possible from a water source and the disposal fields should not be located in a low, damp ground. The drier the soil, the better. Incidentally, a lawn which turns brown during the dry weather of summer can frequently be kept green if watered by such a method. The lines of the disposal pipes can be laid in practically any pattern desired. Fan-shaped or with parallel laterals is a favorite one. Here the branches should be so spaced that they are six feet apart. This will give plenty of surrounding earth to absorb the moisture.

In using this system, there are two things to bear in mind. The action that goes on within a septic tank will only dissolve paper of tissue grade. Therefore, old bandages, pieces of absorbent cotton, and the like should go into the incinerator. Otherwise, they will clog the system and a thorough cleaning will be imperative. Secondly, the leaders which care for the water from the eaves cannot be connected to it, as entirely too much water would flow into the tank during storms.

However, there are several ways of taking care of the water shed by roofs during heavy or protracted rains. In some localities where the supply of water is excessively hard or is so meager that it is not sufficient for all household purposes, pipes from the eaves are connected with an underground cistern, thus conserving the prized rain water. Otherwise, the common practice is simply to equip leaders or down-spouts with "quarter-bend" sections at the lower ends to keep water away from the foundation. This is a cheap and easy way; but if the land does not slope away from the house enough so that this water drains rapidly, pools and mud puddles are the result. Worse still, water may filter through foundation walls and leave a small lake in the cellar after every heavy rain. The disadvantages of the latter are obvious.

The remedy is a dry well for each down-spout. They are simple and inexpensive, being small pits dug six to ten feet away from foundation walls and reaching below the frost line. They are filled to a depth of about two feet with broken stone, fragments of brick, or like material and connected with the down-spouts by glazed tile pipes. A cover of roofing paper is added and the earth then replaced. The rain water is thus absorbed below ground, instead of being left to wear small gullies into an otherwise well-kept lawn.

Sometimes the contour of land about the house is such that it resembles a relief map of the Finger Lake country after each heavy rain or spring freshet. Subsurface drainage is the answer. In other words, a line of land tile like the fields of the septic tank. Through it this mislocated water may drain into a dry well, open ditch, or the gutter along the highway.

Several years ago, highway improvement presented us with such a problem. The road gang put in a culvert through which flowed the drainage from a hill on the opposite side of the road. There was no redress from the Town Fathers. Technically ours was farm land and the established custom was that highway water could wander as it would and drain as natural slope dictated. It was be flooded or do something. A subsurface drain, some fifty feet long and connected with the gutter of an intersecting road, took care of the lawn. For the rest of the water to which we were made heir by the same fit of highway betterment, two local odd-job specialists dug an open trench across a little-used field. It terminated at an old subsurface drainage line constructed years ago when some one, who had the gift, brought forth fine crops of corn, potatoes, and beans there.

There is another drainage problem that concerns mosquitoes, most exasperating of all summer pests. These insects fly but short distances. Marshy land and stagnant pools are their breeding places. If the latter cannot be drained, oil spraying is the alternative and that is work for a professional. Again an old rubbish heap, replete with tin cans and other discards that will hold water, offers more encouragement to mosquitoes than is generally realized. Cart all such rubbish away or bury it; then you can drink your after-dinner coffee in peace on terrace or lawn, or enjoy the coolness of evening dew after a blistering hot day in the city.

# CHAPTER XI

## DECORATIONS AND FURNISHINGS

The decorations and furnishings of a house depend largely on its style of architecture and the owner's taste. Further, if in any doubt, it is better to do too little than too much. Under such circumstances, too, an interior decorator is helpful; but don't dump your problem in her lap and take a trip somewhere. When you return, a beautifully decorated and furnished house, correct in every detail, may greet you. There may even be a few pieces of the furniture you brought from the city home scattered about, but it won't be your house because you will have done nothing except foot the bill.

Homes evolve. They are not pulled, rabbit-like, out of a hat. When you build a house, the architect makes it yours by getting a word picture of your ideas and pulling them down to earth in a series of business-like blueprints. If your ideas regarding decoration are nebulous, a good interior decorator can help to make them concrete. Do not depend on her completely, however, because you are anxious that this country home should be just right and you are afraid of making mistakes. There is nothing final about them and it is better to make a few and have a place that seems like your own home, rather than attain perfection and find your family wandering around the rooms with that impersonal, slightly bored look worn by the average visitor to a "perfect home" display in a department store.

The early American was not afraid of color in his home. His fondness for it is evidenced by 17th and 18th century rooms on display in various museums throughout the country and in the growing number of house museums that have been restored to original condition. Looking at a few of these will help to crystallize your own ideas. You will notice that their furnishings are by no means limited to the year in which they were built or even the century. A good example of this is to be found in a late 17th century house museum, known as Marlpit Hall, located on Kings Highway, Middletown, New Jersey. Here two nationalities actually mingle, since the exterior with its details of roof and gable windows and two-part doors show the Dutch influence, while the woodwork within is English in feeling. It is not a very large house but every room has a different color scheme. The restorers discovered the original colors and reproduced them; now the old blue-green, light pink, apple green, yellow, tones of red, and the like form a perfect background for the furnishings which date from late in the 17th century until well into the 18th.

For instance, in the dining room a gate-leg table of the Puritan years has settled down comfortably with a set of Windsor chairs that are probably a hundred years younger. Other rooms are furnished with William and Mary and Queen Anne pieces so arranged as to appear to be waiting for the owners of Marlpit Hall, in its heyday, to come back. Upstairs are bedrooms with four-post beds of varying ages mingled with other furnishings that are in harmony, though not necessarily of the same period.

This is a very fair example of an Early American home where two or more generations were born, lived, and died. In those days the average citizen did not discard his home furnishings just because they went out of style. He moved them to less important rooms and bought as he could afford of new pieces made "in the neatest and latest fashion."

The home owner today can well plan to use what he has, making a few additions as he and his house become better acquainted. If he has a number of Oriental rugs and some member of his family has a fixed idea that those of the hooked variety are the only kind suitable for a country home, let him buy one or two good hooked rugs, in the interests of peace, and lay them down with his Orientals. Both will be found in harmony because both have the same basic idea, skillful weaving of colors into a distinct but variegated pattern. Besides, the American colonists, industrious as they were, did not depend solely on the work of their hands for floor coverings and other accessories. Oriental rugs or Turkey carpets, as they were then called, were used here in the late 17th and early 18th centuries. They were popular in England, also, as is shown by Hogarth's drawings.

In fact, most house furnishings are surprisingly adaptable. As with people, it is largely a matter of bringing out their pleasing traits and subduing their unattractive aspects. A quaint piece of bric-a-brac that was a misfit in the city apartment may look just right on the corner of the living room mantel in your country home. The old spode platter that reposed almost forgotten on the top shelf of a closet may come into its own on the Welsh dresser of your dining room. The same holds with pictures, mirrors, and clocks.

As for furniture, don't discard a comfortable piece that you like just because it doesn't seem to fit into the scheme of decoration. A chair or a sofa that appears to quarrel violently with all other pieces in a room can often be made to conform by a change in upholstery, or in cases of extreme ugliness, with a slip cover of heavy chintz, denim, or rep.

**TRUE EIGHTEENTH CENTURY SIMPLICITY. NOW THE AUTHOR'S DIN-ING ROOM**

*Photo by John Runyn*

"You see that chair," said one country house owner, a few months after settling in his new home. "Sallie has thrown out every stick of furniture we had when we first went to housekeeping except that. She keeps moving it around from one spot to another but so far has kept it because I like a comfortable chair to drop down in when I come home at night. If I find it gone some day I shall know it is time for me to move on also."

The piece was an average example of the overstuffed, leather-upholstered era. It is still part of the family furnishings but it has merged quietly and inoffensively with its better born companions. Plain muslin has taken the place of the leather and over it has been fitted a heavy slip cover of sage green rep. No one exclaims over its beauty but everybody sits in it, even the most ardent admirer of the delicate Hepplewhite side chair standing nearby.

This brings us to the question of whether the additions in furniture should be antiques, reproductions, or modern pieces. Again, this depends on the type of house and the taste of those who occupy it. The person who buys or builds the salt box or similar type of cottage will naturally want the furnishings in keeping. Consciously or unconsciously, he will lean towards antiques. Further, those that look best in the 18th or early 19th century farm cottage are not necessarily expensive. Simple pine pieces, made by the village cabinet-maker or, sometimes, by an ingenious farmer in his leisure hours; Windsor and slat-back chairs; low four-post beds; trestle or tuckaway tables; even an occasional Victorian piece; all, if on simple lines, fit into such a house as though made for it.

One of the many advantages of furnishing with antiques is that there is nothing final about them. If you buy a piece at a proper price and after due time do not like it or it fails to fit into your decorative scheme, you can sell for as much as you paid for it and often a little more. On the other hand, new furniture or reproductions become merely second-hand pieces as soon as you have bought and put them to use. Only at distinct financial loss can you change them in six months or a year for others. That is a good commercial reason for the growing tendency to furnish with antiques. We believe, however, that the real reason is the effect of individuality gained by the use of pieces made by old craftsmen a century or more ago when things were built to last and mass production and obsolescence were unknown terms.

Several years ago, a family bought a house of the type prevalent in the region of Cape Cod, Massachusetts, "as a summer shack for three or four months in the year." The floors with their wide boards were simply scrubbed, waxed, and left in the natural tone taken on by old wood in the course of a hundred and fifty years. All trim and paneling were painted a soft apple green, and walls and ceilings throughout were calcimined a deep cream color. Curtains of unbleached muslin were hung at the small, many-paned windows. The furnishings came out of the attic of their Boston home where the contents of a great-grandfather's New Hampshire farmhouse had been stored.

These were the average accumulation of family possessions from the turn of the 19th century down through the Civil War period. There was a pine tavern table, 17th century in feeling but made nearly two hundred years later. It had been used in the summer kitchen and bore the scars of harsh treatment. A skillful cabinet-maker restored it to a condition suitable for a dining table. At this point, the antiquarian of the family spoke wistfully of "some nice little rod-back Windsors that Cousin Julie made off with" when the old homestead was broken up some twenty years and how they would be "just right for dining room chairs here."

But all were agreed that the attic contents were to furnish forth the Cape Cod cottage with no unnecessary additions. Here were eight cane-seated chairs of the late Empire years. Four had been painted a dirty brown to simulate black walnut; four represented the white enamel blight which, in turn, had chipped enough to display the "grained" painting of the golden oak years beneath. A scraper applied to a leg revealed the mellow tone of honey-colored maple. Patience and paint remover did the rest. Brought up in the natural finish, they blended beautifully with the old pine table and have been much admired. Yet they were only near-antiques, made by early factory methods about 1850.

So it went. Old pine bureaus, an under-eaves bed, one or two four-posters, late but with simple urn-shaped finials and still covered with the old New England red filler, two or three cherry light stands, and several slat-back chairs went far towards furnishing the bedrooms. The living room, in spite of two or three good tables and ladder-back and Windsor armchairs, appeared to be threatened with a warring element in the shape of a red plush Victorian sofa and matching armchair. Both were ugly but comfortable. Chintz slip covers changed them from blatant monstrosities to background blending items of hominess.

Skillful grouping, plenty of color, and simplicity produced a highly pleasing whole that caused more than one guest to exclaim, "These things look as though they grew in the house." Yet there was not a piece of museum quality in the lot. Many of them could not even be classed as antiques. They were simply the kind of things that the original owner of the house and his descendants would have been apt to accumulate and use through the years. But it is those plus the associations, real or imaginary, that make the difference between a home and a house. The original owner could, of course, have owned finer pieces such as a butterfly table, a maple or cherry highboy, a high-post bed with hangings of crewel-work, a small curly maple and mahogany sideboard, various chests of drawers and light stands made of cherry and neatly ornamented with inlay. Country cabinet-makers were as fine artists as those who catered to the urban taste but their public was satisfied with simple pieces and they wrought accordingly.

Calcimined walls and near-antique furnishings are, naturally, not the only means of producing a homey effect. Their chief merit lies in the fact that they are effective, inexpensive, and easily changed. No matter how pleasing the tone, plain calcimined walls will probably pall after a while, but by that time the home owner will know whether paper or paint is the better treatment. With an old house, either is historically correct. The earliest were, of course, primitive affairs with walls of rough plaster or feather-board paneling in natural wood color. By the 18th century, paint was already being used for decorating both. Here the wall treatment was not limited to a plain color but was varied by stencil designs. A geometric pattern was usual. Then came wall papers of geometric or scenic design.

Thus, it is for the householder to decide just what manner of decoration he wishes to live with. For instance, a paneled room may be finished in the natural wood or painted. The latter was customary in colonial days as life became easier and money more plentiful. Personally we consider painted paneling, trim, and other woodwork pleasanter and less monotonous to live with day in and day out but that is a matter of individual taste. In the last analysis it is not what his neighbor likes, it is what the home owner himself wants to live with that really matters.

In choosing wall paper, one is limited by the type and size of room to be so decorated. You may have a weakness for the old French scenic papers depicting, in large squares, historic or sporting events. These are most effective in the large central halls of the more formal country home but produce a distinctly odd appearance in the tiny, low-ceilinged rooms of the story-and-a-half farmhouse. Here small patterns and designs that tend to make the rooms look larger must rule.

Over-fussy curtains and draperies at the windows should also be avoided. We well remember an otherwise charming little place where the use of color and type of furnishings was most skillful. One experienced a curious sense of gloom and stuffiness, though, even at midday. A glance at the windows explained it. They were of the 18th century farmhouse type and into their 42 by 28 inch dimensions had been crowded the modern roller shade, fussy ruffled dimity curtains and heavily lined chintz draperies surmounted by a six-inch valance! With all these, the aperture left for light and air was limited indeed.

An able interior decorator could have controlled the over-zealous drapery buyer or she could have found out for herself by a little independent study of proper window treatment for a house of that type. In other words, whatever the kind of house, remember that windows are intended to let in light and air. Both constitute excellent reasons for living in the country. Proper curtains and draperies lend a softening and pleasing effect but, as in a stage setting, they are only props and must not be allowed to dominate the scene.

Further, in furnishing or decorating any house it is an excellent idea to try and visualize the type of furnishings two or three generations living there would normally have accumulated. We have already alluded at some length to the farm cottage type because, like the common people, they are more numerous. But in the old country neighborhoods there was nearly always the man of affairs who knew how to make money and was prone to build a house "as handsome as his purse could afford." He was the squire of his vicinity and his house surpassed all others in size and ornamental detail. If you have acquired such a house, its furnishings must be in accord. Handsome antiques and ambitious reproductions go well in such a setting. Or it may be that your fancy runs to an ultra modern structure with interior decorations and furnishings in keeping. Your house is then its own ancestor and only time will determine whether such a scheme wears well.

Whatever you choose, take the furnishings best suited, arrange them as pleases you, and proceed to live with them. If you like the general effect and are one of those people who like things to stay put, probably one can enter your living room fifteen years hence and find the wing chair from the Maritime Provinces still standing in the northeast corner with a small tavern table on the right; the hooked rug with geometric center still in front of the fireplace; the Sheraton table with mirror over it at its accustomed place between the two south windows; and so forth.

On the other hand, if you are of the restless type, instead of throwing everything out and beginning over again, you will have periodic attacks of rearranging, realigning certain accessories, adding something new, or discarding some item bought in an emergency for something more in keeping with your changing ideas or manner of living. We confess that this is one of our pleasantest pastimes. It takes very little to start us off. An old Pennsylvania Dutch cupboard, stripped down to the original blue and inducted into an apple-green dining room, obviously calls for a fine orgy with paint and whitewash; a gilded Sheraton mirror or another oil painting involves general commotion and often complete rearrangement of the living room. All this is very painful for those who don't like change; but, for us, it helps to answer the question so often propounded by innocent city visitors, "What do you do with yourselves in such a quiet spot?"

# CHAPTER XII

## THE FACTORY PART OF THE HOUSE

The Early American kitchen was the most important room in the house. Here the family spent most of its waking hours. Here the food was cooked, served, and eaten; the spinning and weaving done; the candles for lighting the house poured into molds. It was the warmest room in winter and around its hearth the family gathered both for work and recreation.

Cheerful and pleasant it undoubtedly was, but there was little idea of making work easy or saving steps. Today we may furnish our living rooms in the 18th century manner, put 17th century dressers in our dining rooms, and hang Betty lamps and other quaint devices around the fireplace; but when it comes to the kitchen, we step forward into the 20th century and are well content. We have heard of enthusiasts who occasionally cook an entire meal in a fireplace and insist that it is far superior to any done by modern methods; but even these devotees of old ways pale at the thought of three meals a day, three hundred and sixty-five days in the year, so prepared.

Today's kitchen, stripped of accessories and talking points, is essentially a laboratory where semi-prepared food stuffs are processed for consumption. The automobile industry has demonstrated to the nation what remarkable things can be done by having labor conditions and proper tools on a logical train of production. With no waste of human effort, no running back and forth, work starts at one end of the assembly chain, and off the other, in about two hours, comes a new car. In the same way, a properly planned kitchen eliminates waste steps and, with plenty of light and air, becomes a pleasant place to work.

In this domestic laboratory, one expects, of course, to find a cook stove of some sort, a sink, a refrigerator, a kitchen cabinet or compounding bench, a table, and plenty of storage space. With the assembly idea in mind, have these so planned that the work of cooking three meals a day progresses logically from the service or delivery entrance to the doorway of the dining room. Be sure, too, that added working space is available in the event of dinner parties or larger forms of entertainment. The saving on tempers, fine china, and glass will be well worth it. In other words, have this most important working room compact but not too small.

As an example we cite another of our own errors in judgment. Having been brought up in a house with a large old-fashioned kitchen where the luckless cook walked miles in performing her culinary duties, we went to the other extreme. The room originally designed for the kitchen with its large old fireplace and sunny southern exposure was immediately chosen for the dining room. Directly back of it was the old pantry which, without benefit of architectural advice, we decided to fit up as a kitchen. It was a good idea except for the fact that the room was really too small, especially for the type of hospitality that rules in the country. To be sure, by moving a partition a little and by remodeling a small lean-to that adjoined it, sufficient storage and working space was added to make conditions tolerable; but it is at best a makeshift and the answer is, eventually, a properly designed service wing, architecturally in keeping with the 18th century but mechanically modern. Even under these makeshift conditions, however, the assembly idea has been followed and this somewhat mitigates the drawback of contracted space.

The most important tool in a kitchen is obviously the cooking range. Here the country dweller has a choice of bottled gas, electricity, or oil as fuels. What he decides to use may depend on personal preference, availability, or cost of installing and operating. Where service is dependable and a reasonable cooking rate prevails, there is no better method of cooking than by electricity. Clean, odorless and easily regulated, its advantages are obvious. But no electric light and power company can afford to run its cables underground in the country. The service lines are on poles and extend over a large area. Nature has no regard for the convenience of either the company or its patrons. A thunderbolt may knock out a transformer, or a tree may be blown down and carry nearby electric lines with it. Repair men are continually on the job with a well-run company and work speedily and faithfully but they cannot be everywhere at once. Service may be interrupted for ten minutes or for several hours. In such emergencies, it is well to have a stop gap, such as an inexpensive two-burner oil stove. It may not be used more than twice a year but it is there when needed.

The devotees of the tank gas method of cooking are many. It works the same as gas from city mains except that your supply is piped in from an individual tank which is installed outside the house and replenished monthly by the company supplying such fuel. The initial cost plus installation and operation about equals that of electricity but no cataclysm of nature will cause it to fail.

Cheapest of all is the kerosene oil stove. These range all the way from the modest two-burner table stove to the pretentious six-burner type with insulated oven and porcelain finish. Gasoline burning ranges are also to be had on this order. The initial cost of even the most elaborate oil or gasoline stove is considerably less than for one designed for either electricity or bottled gas and the expense of operation is also less. But they have certain disadvantages. With the best of management there is a slight odor. If out of adjustment they smoke or go out and they are unpleasant to clean. Further, although we struggled with one for seven years, we never found any satisfactory means of broiling meat with oil as a fuel.

No family relishes the idea of having porterhouse or sirloin steaks taken right out of their lives, so some other device is necessary, such as a charcoal broiler or the old-fashioned, long-handled broiler held over the fireplace coals or, in winter, those of the furnace. One may argue brightly that meat cooked by these primitive methods has a superior flavor, but it is definitely veering away from the assembly idea and most certainly does not make for harmony in the kitchen. If a charcoal broiler is employed, somehow it never reaches the proper state of incandescence at the right time. If the fireplace is the scene of operation, it is invariably a roaring inferno at the time the steak should be cooked. One waits for the desired bed of coals, of course, while ominous head shakings and rumblings from the kitchen proclaim that the rest of the dinner is done, is dried up, is ruined.

Twenty years ago coal or wood burning stoves were usual in country homes. They were disagreeable to tend and in summer made an uncomfortably hot kitchen. But that same heat was most acceptable in winter weather. For a kitchen not too well heated by the main house system, there are ranges that combine coal and electricity. Thus, in winter they serve the double purpose of a cooking tool and heat producing unit and also help reduce the electric light bill at the season of the year when it tends to be heaviest.

Where electricity is available, the problem of refrigeration is simple. Of course, the initial cost of a good electric refrigerator may easily be more than double that of the ordinary icebox, but the cost of operation is very small and food losses are materially cut down. The old method of refrigeration calls for only a moderate outlay for a box, but delivering ice three or four times a week to the average country home involves heavy overhead for the local ice dealer and he must therefore charge accordingly. If one must depend on ice, however, there is an improved box now on the market so constructed that it needs to be filled but once a week. It operates on much the same principle as the mechanical box as far as keeping an even temperature is concerned.

With the various storage cupboards, closets, and cabinets that make up the furnishings of this culinary assembly plant, there are sundry built-in units, widely pictured, written about, and advertised. What type you will have is a matter of personal taste. The main thing is to be sure they are well built and conveniently located. The kitchen sink may also be of any type you prefer but let there be light where it is hung. A window directly over it will make for cleaner dishes as well as less breakage. Another ounce of prevention for the latter is considered by many to be the sink lined with monel metal. It is fairly soft and yielding so that a cup or plate is not readily shattered if accidentally dropped in it. With porcelain sinks, one may use a rubber mat designed for the purpose or one can be careful.

**ENTIRELY NEW, BUT WITH ALL THE CHARM OF AN OLD HOUSE**

*Robertson Ward, architect. Photo by Samuel H. Gottscho*

If the service wing plans do not include a laundry, a set tub with cover forming one of the drain boards is practical for the occasional small pieces washed at home. Along with the sink may be installed an electric dishwasher, depending, of course, on whether the family considers its benefits equal to the expense involved. If mother is to do the work, it may be warranted; but where her efforts are limited to one or two sketchy meals on Thursdays and Sunday evenings, one might well interview the person who is monitor of the service wing the bulk of the time. Dishwashers, cake mixers, complicated fruit juice extractors, and similar gadgets are all excellent but they are not essential. Many servants do not even want them.

A few years ago we tried to introduce an orange squeezer designed to hang on the wall and operate somewhat on the principle of a pencil sharpener. We showed it to our houseman who regarded it glumly. "I'll try to use it if you insist," he finally said, "but I can work faster with that glass one from the ten cent store." These little playthings are all right but you can seldom get the help to use them. A kitchen should be well equipped with standard implements and cooking utensils, but before putting in expensive labor-saving devices one should be sure that they really save work and that the proposed operator will appreciate them enough to make their purchase advisable.

The essentials of a kitchen are plenty of light and air; enough space for working under all conditions; well arranged and adequate equipment; pleasing, easily cleaned wall surfaces and floor; and plenty of hot water. There are several methods of obtaining an adequate supply of the latter. It is automatically taken care of where the house is heated by an oil burning system. With a coal burning steam or hot water plant, there is now a cylinder that can be attached to the boiler below the water level. In it there is a coil of copper pipe through which circulates the domestic hot water supply. This works admirably. There is always a sufficient supply but it is never so overheated as to scald the heedless person who plunges a hand under a boiling stream of water.

During the warm months, however, a supplementary means of heating water must be at hand. Electric water heating, again, involves the least supervision and is to be recommended if one can get a low enough rate. The initial expense is a sizable item, though; and if operated at the usual rate per kilowatt hour, the monthly charge can easily be double that of other fuels. But many companies make a special rate for such devices and under such circumstances the operating costs compare favorably with those of coal and oil.

Another excellent device is the little coal stove built especially for the purpose. It requires only a small amount of fuel daily but, of course, must be faithfully tended. This type of stove may also be adapted for burning range oil. Here the drudgery of shoveling in coal and taking out ashes is replaced by that of daily filling the two-gallon oil tank that feeds it, periodic cleaning of wicks and burners, and consistent adjusting of burner and draft to meet changing weather conditions.

There are also the kerosene oil heaters having a copper coil through which the water circulates in heating. These may or may not be equipped with an automatic attachment. They likewise require daily filling and occasional cleaning of both wick and copper coil. They are easier to adjust than the other variety but the action of the blue flame on the copper coil causes a slight disintegration which over a long period of time may cause a leak. When that happens no mending is possible, not even of a temporary nature. The family goes without hot water until a new coil is put in or a complete new heater substituted. Obsolescence is a term high in favor with American industry; and only too often when one goes seeking a new part for a machine with a decade of good service to its credit, one is met with, "Oh, we don't make that model any more. We might be able to locate a stray coil but it would take about two or three weeks." The disgusted home owner naturally goes out and buys another kind of heater, one without a copper coil.

Whether or not a laundry is part of the service wing depends, of course, on how much of that type of work is to be done at home. There are two points of view here. Some households prefer to scoop the family linen into a bag, make a list, and hand it over to a commercial laundry. Others find a dependable laundress nearby or provide facilities for doing the work at home. The clear air of the country and easy drying conditions influence many towards the latter course.

Like the kitchen, the room set aside for this purpose should have good light and air as well as easily cleaned wall and floor surfaces. There should be at least two tubs as well as a washing machine and a small ironing machine. There should also be space provided for indoor drying of clothes since, even in the country, a week of stormy weather is not unheard of. Some kind of a stove is also necessary for any needed boiling of clothes, making starch, or the like.

Servants' quarters should be cheerful, light, airy in summer and comfortably warm in winter. They may be part of the service wing; they may be on a separate floor of the main section of the house; or, if the garage is part of the house, located over that. For best results they should not be in too close proximity to the rest of the family. In the country, servants are more confined to the scene of their labors than in the city. Consequently they need and like a certain amount of privacy as well as a place to relax and see their friends. In addition to bedrooms and bath, a sitting room of some kind is most practical. It need not be large or expensively furnished. A few comfortable chairs, a table or two, possibly a desk and a good reading lamp will suffice. A small radio also adds to the general contentment. In summer if the service wing boasts a screened porch so much the better. If not, some shady nook or arbor nearby where they may rest or read during their spare time may mark the difference between sullen service, frequent change of personnel, and the perfect servant who remains year after year.

# CHAPTER XIII
## PETS AND LIVESTOCK

Few country households are content with a bowl of goldfish. Something a little more responsive is demanded where the peace and quiet of nature press so close. A cat to drowse on the hearth or catch an occasional mouse; a dog to accompany one on walks and greet the head of the house ecstatically each evening; these, of course, are the most obvious and popular pets. Both can be and are kept in city apartments and suburban homes but their natural habitat is the open country.

Whether one or both become part of your household is, of course, a matter of personal inclination. There are those who have an intense aversion for cats. There are fanatical bird lovers who argue that because they once knew a cat which killed a bird, the entire feline family should be wiped out. However, from the number of sleek specimens seen dozing on porch or terrace through the countryside, it is safe to assume that the average household harbors at least one cat. There is no room here for a treatise on why people keep cats. Besides, we do not know. We only know that cats were always about the place when we were young and that some sixteen years ago we rescued a half starved Maltese kitten from a city pavement and kept her until she died of old age about a year ago. She had beautiful green eyes and a very short temper. She also upset several preconceived theories. One is that a cat is attached to a place rather than people and that it is difficult if not impossible to take it along when moving to an old place. Our cat was approaching middle age when we acquired our country home. Yet after a few inquiring meows and a minute inspection of the new place, she settled down contentedly. Further, during the years that followed, she made at least two trips a year to the city for sojourns of varying lengths. Inquiry among other cat owners has revealed that this is not at all extraordinary. In fact, this type of animal can become just as attached to its owner as the more flattering and responsive dog.

Nor do all cats kill birds. The average house cat is too indolent to hunt anything. Our own imperfect but individualistic animal was a mighty hunter of field mice but showed little or no interest in the birds flying about above her. They have built their nests for years in arbor and summer house unmolested. But a real killer of birds is hard to dissuade. One can of course remove the bird from its jaws and administer a sound whipping but it is by no means certain that anything much is accomplished by so doing. One cannot argue with a cat. He is the one animal man has not been able to subdue. Possibly therein lies his fascination. Also, barring a few bad habits, he is little trouble and is a distinct ornament.

The dog can be a faithful companion or the worst pest on earth. Which he is, depends on his environment and training. He may be had in many breeds and sizes from the most expensive and delicate specimens down to the mongrel with a League of Nations ancestry. Incidentally, the most benign and intelligent of dogs is often some middle-aged hound of doubtful lineage who can tell your blue ribbon winner how to get about in the canine circles of the countryside.

Pick the breed you prefer but have it in scale with your place. You may have had a secret longing for a St. Bernard or a Great Dane but if you have settled your family in a little saltbox house, it is going to be a little crowded when something only slightly smaller than a Shetland pony starts padding restlessly up and down stairs or flings his weary length down in the middle of the living room rug where you must walk around or over him to turn on the radio or answer the telephone.

One member of our family has always wanted a cheetah or hunting leopard. This desire is likely to go unfulfilled. These beasts are easily domesticated and are gentle and affectionate. They appear to have the best characteristics of both cat and dog. They are no more expensive than many a thoroughbred dog. Yet we shall not have one. Not only is the climate of Westchester County, New York, too unlike that of their native India for them to thrive, but consider the task of soothing terrified tradesmen and casual visitors. One may explain that although appearances are against him he is not really a leopard but just an overgrown cat. They will not believe it. They will not even hear because they will be a mile down the road.

Other people must be considered even in the country. So pick your dog and train him up in the way he should go. You may prefer one of the terrier breeds. They are bright and lively and make good pets but must be taught not to dig holes in the carefully groomed lawn. It is as natural for them to delve for underground animals as for a setter or spaniel to flush birds. Retrievers are usually gentle, well disposed animals and not only make good pets but are excellent in a family where hunting is a diversion. Very popular just now in this class are the spaniels, especially the cockers. They have beauty, an affectionate disposition, are most intelligent and are excellent watch dogs. They fit into nearly any household large or small.

With the larger dogs there is, of course, the collie as well as his ancestor the old-fashioned shepherd. Here we would say a good word for a much-maligned dog, the police or German shepherd. Only recently since the Seeing Eye has demonstrated their keen intelligence and sense of responsibility in guiding their blind owners, have they begun to come into their own again. Even now there is an impression abroad in the land that they, like the timber wolf they so much resemble but are *not* descended from, are sly treacherous brutes with a particular delight in taking a piece out of the unwary stranger. It is true that when first brought to this country they had no little trouble in adapting themselves to conditions here. In their native Germany they were what their name implies and as working dogs covered miles daily. They ate coarse food and slept in the open either on the ground itself or a small heap of straw. Obviously such a dog cannot be shut up in cramped quarters and given almost no exercise without his disposition being somewhat affected. They are highly intelligent animals and for the country dweller with two or more acres, make affectionate and satisfactory pets. They have a keen sense of guardianship, are fine watch dogs and show but little tendency to roam.

The latter is an excellent trait for if you wish to remain on moderately pleasant terms with your neighbors, train your dog or dogs to stay home. Worrying the cat of the man who lives just at the bend in the road to the south, or killing the chickens of the neighbor to the north, will not aid in establishing friendly relations. Barking at passing cars is not commendable nor is the tipping over of a neighbor's garbage can and scattering the contents about. These are bad habits and should be corrected if your pet is to be any real comfort to you. Patient and intelligent training will mark the difference between a friendly well-mannered dog and a spoiled brute that even your most humane friends yearn to cuff.

When it comes to the matter of other livestock in this venture of farming-in-the-little, the new owner is either treading unknown or forgotten ground. Dogs and cats, even canaries and white rats, were familiar enough in the city. He has read books on their care and training. He has consulted veterinarians and fanciers but until now the sources of his daily bottle of milk or his carton of graded eggs have been matters of indifference. The venture with livestock may begin with chickens and end with saddle horses, but it is nothing for the uninitiate to enter into lightly or unadvisedly. Personally, we prefer to let the farmer down at the end of the lane wrestle with the recalcitrant hen and temperamental cow. He has summered and wintered with them for years and knows the best and the worst of them. If there is a way to make them worth their keep, he knows it. If his cow generously gives twelve quarts of milk and we can use but two, it is no concern of ours what becomes of the other ten.

For the country dweller, who feels that life is not complete without livestock of some sort and follows that by acquiring a barnyard menagerie, we would recommend that he enter upon his course cautiously. This is assuming that he knows little or nothing of farming either by theory or practice. If, on the other hand, he has been reared on a farm, he understands perfectly how to care for the various animals and the labor entailed in doing so. He is in no need of any admonition from us, and who are we to offer it? But for the average person who is just beginning his experiment in country living, a few chickens are suggested for the initial attempt. There are two ways to embark on this. With either, it is well to subscribe to a good farm journal. Consult that or the farmer down the road as to breed. As rank outsiders we suggest a well established and hardy kind.

Then, the easiest way for the novice would probably be to buy full-grown chickens that are just beginning to lay. They are old enough to know their way about and any dry, well ventilated shelter that is proof against thieving skunks, weasels and similar wild life, will be adequate for them along with a chicken run with a high enough fence to keep them within bounds. For this type of fowl is no respecter of property. Not only does it take delight in working havoc with its owner's flower beds and borders but those of his neighbor as well.

They also eat incessantly. The optimistic friend who has never kept chickens, but thinks it a marvelous idea, will tell you that scraps from the table will take care of all that and even save you the garbage collector's fee. Such a person is still living back in the 1890's when food was cheap and seven course dinners and hearty suppers were the rule. Today's orange skins and banana peels are no diet even for a chicken. So, one must buy feed for them. This should be offset in a measure by the eggs normally laid by well-fed and tended pullets. Also as time goes on and setting hens hatch chickens, which in turn become eventually broilers or fresh producers of eggs, according to results you will decide whether or not you want to continue in the chicken business.

Another method widely advocated is to buy week-old chicks from a mail order house or other firm dealing in such stock and bring them up without aid of a mother hen to gather them under her wings. Here a brooder is necessary since the chicks are of tender age and must be kept warm. These brooders are of varying sizes and prices and may be had from the same mail order houses that are glad to sell the chicks as well. This is more complicated than the other old-fashioned method but a little guidance from some one understanding the procedure along with consistent care on your part will probably bring a majority of your brood to broiler size.

Taking on a cow to support is a much more serious thing. Not only does a well-bred, tuberculin-tested animal cost a fair sum to acquire, but she must be comfortably housed in a clean, comfortable cow barn. Bulletins from the Department of Agriculture will give the requirements not only for her shelter but for her proper care. She needs at least two acres of pasturage and this can't be all stones and bushes. She must be milked morning and evening without fail and at regular hours by some one who knows how. She must be groomed. Her stable must be cleaned regularly. When the yearly calf is born one must sit up nights with her. All this, if she is to remain in good condition. In gratitude for it she will give milk, three or four times as much as a small household can consume. Possibly a market can be found for this excess or one can turn to butter making and add a pig to the barnyard family. Even this accommodating scavenger cannot live by skim milk alone but must have it augmented by corn or prepared feed. He must also have proper shelter and a run. Thus does one thing lead to another, once one gets beyond the chicken stage of farming. It is obviously nothing for the daily commuter to attempt unless he is prepared to pay for the services of a competent hired man.

Farming even on the smallest scale is a full-time job in itself. The tired business man will find it a toil or a pleasure. The daily chores involved are relentless and unending. A business appointment in town is no excuse for their non-fulfillment. They must be done at a regular time, if not by you by some one else. Of course, with a family where there are three or more small children, keeping a cow can be both practical and economical. With the normal table and cooking uses the milk given can be consumed without difficulty. Further, the expense of maintaining would probably fall much below the monthly milk bill under such circumstances. For this purpose, select one of the Jersey or Guernsey breed which gives rich milk rather than quantity.

For the family that can afford and enjoy saddle horses, it is pleasant to have them, but with their advent the country home becomes still more complicated. There must be a stable with somebody to tend and groom the horses. They must be exercised too, which means systematic riding rather than an occasional canter on just the ideal day. Also with even one horse, if a need for economy arises it is not always easy to dispense with him. He is flesh and blood and, humanely, you cannot just sell him to the first buyer who presents himself. You must be assured that your mount will be well-treated and not abused. We have known of several instances where a number of excellent saddle horses were given away by owners, who felt that they could no longer afford to buy their oats and hay, but wanted to be sure the animals would be well cared for.

So, before acquiring horses, contemplate the up-keep and make sure you are prepared to maintain them whether business is good, bad, or indifferent. For the first year or two a much wiser course is to turn to the neighborhood riding stable and rent. These have become standard institutions in many vicinities and they frequently afford not only excellent mounts but sound teaching for those who know little or nothing about the finer points of riding.

# CHAPTER XIV

## TIGHTENING FOR WINTER

The wolf of winter was the arresting phrase originated several years ago by no less a practitioner of the art of advertising than Bruce Barton, to drive home the merits of adequate domestic heating. But no matter how efficient your heating system may be, unless the country home has been made ready for the cold months, insufficient heat and excessive fuel bills result.

Against this, there are a number of simple things the home owner may do himself or have done. Nobody begrudges money spent for fuel that keeps the house at a comfortable, even temperature. In the days when six dollars bought a ton of the best anthracite coal and the pea and buckwheat sizes were sold as waste products, it may have been a matter of small importance that certain spots in a house leaked heat and let in cold. Besides, in an era when windows closed tightly with the first cold blasts of fall and remained so until spring, such ventilation was probably a life saver. But at the present high prices for either coal or fuel oil, these points about the house where heat is lost and winter cold crashes the gate should be taken seriously.

With a new house, of course, everything possible in the nature of built-in metal weatherstripping and thoroughly insulated exterior walls were included by the architect when he prepared plans and specifications. But even he may have ignored one of the most practical means of conserving warmth. This is a set of storm windows and doors carefully fitted so they open and shut at will, yet are snug enough so that little cold penetrates. These are remarkable conservers of heat. Measured scientifically, the amount that escapes by radiation through ordinary window glass is amazing. The storm window reduces this to a minor percentage because the dead-air space between the two thicknesses of glass acts as an efficient means of insulation.

Storm doors and windows are now made in stock dimensions that fit practically any frame. Quantity production has made their price so moderate that the saving on fuel for a single winter can exceed their initial cost and the labor of fitting and putting them in place. Such windows and doors should be properly marked, like the screens that replace them in summer, with numbering tacks so that, each fall, they may be put in proper place without confusion. The system is simplicity itself. A duplicate tack bears the same number on the sill of each window and on the upright of each door. This is a real saver of time, for so small a variation as half an inch in width or height can make the difference between doors and windows that really fit and those that leak air. Such proportions vary even with a new house.

The only requisite for such a complement of double doors and windows is a proper place to store them during the summer months. Being largely of glass, if they are not put away carefully, the breakage can be both annoying and needlessly expensive. So it is well to provide a special compartment, located in the garage or other convenient place, where these may be placed when not in use. Similarly, the same section may be used in the winter for door and window screens as well as garden furniture.

Except for the new country house or one that has been completely remodeled or renovated, each succeeding fall brings minor repairs. These ought to be undertaken during those cool crisp days of fall that precede freezing weather and penetrating winter winds. They will vary with age and state of repair but they begin with the cellar and progress upward to the attic. Unless your house is unusually ailing, probably not all of these will be necessary but at least there should be a careful examination and diagnosis. Here is the list.

Repoint the foundations, inside and out, with a rich cement mortar to seal any cracks through which the wind might penetrate. A late October or early November day when there is a high wind is ideal for this work. As one goes over the inside of the foundation, the searching cold blasts will reveal the crevices that need attention. Mark each one with a wooden splinter as fast as they are found. When all four walls have been thoroughly inspected, the work of closing these cracks can be done as a single operation. Except for a solid brick or stone house, inspect the point at which the sills rest on the foundation walls. The fillet of mortar may have come loose or cracked in places. Any such breaks should be repaired.

Before leaving the cellar notice the windows. Does cold air leak through joints of sash and frame? If so, make them tight with batten strips or, if very loose, calk them with oakum. The window through which coal is delivered, of course, cannot be sealed so thoroughly as it may have to be opened now and then for additional fuel. Weatherstripping it as well as the hatchway door is advisable.

**SNOW HAS DIGNITY, BUT IS THE HOUSE SNUG AND WARM?**

*Photo by Samuel H. Gottscho*

Some houses built on side-hill sites have at least one cellar wall more exposed than the rest. Where this condition exists, it is a real economy to cover the inside of it with insulating material. Either special plastering or fiber-insulating board can be used, as individual conditions warrant. At the same time any water pipe that is close to an outside wall should either be re-located or insulated, lest it freeze some day when it is abnormally cold or a high wind is blowing. Freezing cold air blowing through a fine crack in an exterior wall acts about as does the flame of a welder's torch, only in the reverse. The flame cuts by melting; the cold air solidifies the water in a pipe and sometimes does it so thoroughly that a cracked pipe is the result.

From the cellar one now goes to the attic. Are windows in place here and weather tight? How about end walls and the under sides of roof? If not insulated, your house can lose a quantity of heat at these points. Remember, heat rises and, after a storm, if the snow on the roof of your house melts quicker than on those of your neighbors, it is a clear demonstration that you are wasting heat by letting it ooze through certain minute apertures. Another way to combat this upward radiation is to pour a loose, featherlike insulating material into the space between the attic flooring and the plaster of the bedroom ceilings. As it comes in bags prepared especially for this purpose and is very light, sometimes it is only necessary to raise a small proportion of the attic floor boards and the insulating material can be spread evenly through these openings.

There remains still a major escape for heat, the fireplaces. If each is equipped, as is customary with all built during the last half century, with a cast-iron damper that closes the throat when not in use, make sure it is in working order. Sometimes such dampers get clogged with soot and fail to close tightly. For older fireplaces the problem varies. Some can have a throat damper installed; others are of such size or shape that it is not practical. With the latter, if the throat is not too large, it is possible to stuff it with tightly packed newspaper, first crumpling the sheets to make them bulky. The large fireplace, once the scene of all family cooking, generally has an opening into the chimney so large that there seems to be but one practical way to treat it. This is the use of the time-tried fire board which fits tightly into the opening of mantel and shuts off the fireplace completely. This causes much lamentation each winter in our own household, as the picturesque effect of the fine old fireplace with swinging crane is blotted out by a none too ornamental expanse of board. But it is so fitted that it can be readily removed any time a fireplace fire is desired. When not in use such a cavernous avenue for escaping heat must, of course, be closed. No heating system can compete with it. Stand beside such a fireplace for a moment and the cold breeze swirling out from it will convince you.

Nothing is more uncomfortable in winter than cold and drafty floors. Much of this can easily be corrected by closing the cracks, usually found in older houses, between flooring and walls at the baseboards. Generally quarter-round molding, carefully fitted and securely nailed is sufficient but occasionally wide, uneven cracks have to be closed with oakum, putty, or crack filler before the molding is put in place. Again, if the cellar has no plaster ceiling, a drafty floor can be remedied by lining the under side of the flooring with felt paper or like material.

Lastly, inspect the heating plant. Has it been cleaned and put in order since last season? If not, it should be done without fail, for no soot-clogged furnace or encrusted boiler can work properly. You are simply wasting fuel and effort if you neglect them.

Out of doors, there are several minor things that can make or mar a winter in the country. Be sure the faucets used for the garden hose are disconnected and drained. There is probably a drain valve in the cellar for this. If your water supply is a shallow well, notice the location of the supply pipe. If it extends to within four or five feet of the top, some sort of covering must be placed over the latter to prevent cold winter winds searching it out. A cover of wall board with a small opening for ventilation is easily fitted to it and will avert later trouble.

It is far from amusing to awake some zero morning and find the house without water because the well pipe has frozen. It can be thawed with a blow pipe but that means calling a plumber or a handy man who happens to have a tool of this sort. One such experience will keep you from forgetting or neglecting to provide a well cover. Similarly, if you are in doubt whether the pipes from water source to house are below the frost line, a carpet of leaves about two inches thick on top of the ground along the course of the water pipe, will obviate any such unhappy event. Thawing a frozen pipe plainly visible in the well is child's play compared to the task of arguing with any underground. Once, such pipes had to wait for nature. Today, they can be thawed very skillfully with special electrical equipment, but not cheaply. The standard charge ranges from $20 up, mostly the latter.

The family living in the country will also find that cold weather puts a great strain on the automobile. A car that has worked perfectly all summer simply refuses to start, and the storage battery that operates the self-starter is exhausted and powerless. The sensible course is to have the car put in condition for winter before the first cold snap congeals the crank-case oil. Replace the latter with one of lighter grade; have the radiator filled with a good anti-freeze in sufficient quantity so that you will be safe on the coldest days against the hazard of a frozen radiator; have the ignition system thoroughly overhauled and new spark points put in the distributor. Most important of all, get a new storage battery if the one you have is more than a few months old.

This course of action saves annoyance, is better for the automobile, and less expensive than calling for garage help some abnormally cold morning when many others are also in trouble and you must wait your turn. Don't take just anybody's advice when changing to lighter and more freely flowing motor oil. Go to the service station handling the make of car you drive and have it done there. They will know which is the right grade. We once almost ruined a car by following a layman's advice. With our own hands we refilled the crank case with oil that was rated as S.A.E. 10 and was perfect for the light car of our well-intentioned adviser. Unhappily the lightest suitable for our make and model was S.A.E. 20, practically twice as heavy. Fortunately we burned no bearings before our error was discovered and so learned a valuable lesson more cheaply than we deserved.

Keeping the radiator protected against freezing is not complicated. Nearly any filling station has the necessary hydrometer. To be sure the anti-freeze liquid has not evaporated unduly, have the radiator contents tested about once in two weeks, particularly after several days of abnormally warm weather. For real safety, it is wise to have any automobile radiator filled with enough of the compound so that its freezing point is fully ten degrees colder than the lowest temperature expected. There are two reasons for this margin. It allows for a slight percentage of evaporation and for a certain peculiarity of country highways. There are sometimes points on the road where, for some reason, the actual temperature is a full five degrees colder than elsewhere. We have seen many cars steaming and boiling in such places. We have once or twice been in the same unhappy situation and know that thawing a radiator so frozen is slow work, requiring blankets and plenty of patience.

A word as to the clothing especially designed for the cold of the country. Wool-lined mittens may seem to hark back to sleighbells and buffalo robes, but driving a spirited span hitched to a cutter was a summer occupation compared to steering an unheated automobile ten miles on a below zero morning with ordinary gloves. Mittens are not graceful but in them the fingers are not confined and therefore do not chill as quickly.

Further, do not scorn the good old-fashioned arctics. Get the high four-buckle kind. They afford real protection against cold and snow and a pair lasts for several years, particularly in the sections of the country where snow and abnormally cold weather are intermittent. Sweaters and woolen mufflers should also be part of the added equipment, for nothing makes for such misery as getting thoroughly chilled for lack of adequate outside clothing. A walk or a drive becomes then just an endurance test.

We have one last warning. The mitten and overshoe theory may seem to you but a sad sign of approaching age and debility—and so none of them for you. Granted they are not needed except for abnormal weather, some bitter cold evening you may arrive home with fingers, or ears, or toes frostbitten. Don't under such circumstances go into a warm room before you have thawed them with snow and vigorous massage. When you do go into the warm atmosphere continue to treat the bite with cloths wrung out in ice water. Otherwise, this simple winter casualty may be as serious and painful as a bad burn.

# CHAPTER XV

## KEEPING HOME FIRES IN THEIR PLACE

In the good old days before the United States had a record of one fire every minute of the twenty-four hours, grandfather and his father before him considered that a good citizen paid his poll tax, served on juries, and patrolled his home for fire. Going to bed without banking fires in stoves and fireplaces was unthinkable. The rest of the household also had a proper respect for lighted candles and other possible fire breeders. Of course, under this simpler mode of living, light and heat were generated within view and what is seen cannot be readily ignored.

Then came the development of modern household conveniences. Furnaces and steam plants took heating below stairs; electricity replaced candles, lamps, and gas fixtures; and the old cook stove gave way to modern ranges of various sorts. The safer and easier the devices, the more human vigilance relaxed. Today, of our half billion dollar fire loss annually, one-fifth of it occurs in the country, and over sixty per cent of residential fires start in the cellar.

Of course, every home has certain fire hazards but they can be reduced to the minimum by a few elemental improvements and precautions. Some call for slight additions to the house equipment; others are simply the old-fashioned art of self-fire policing. This program of little things starts in the cellar and ends in the attic. Here is the list.

Don't let piles of rubbish and papers accumulate in cellar, attic, closets, and like places.

Provide a metal container with hinged cover for storing inflammable polishes, cleaning fluids, chemically treated dust cloths, mops, oily cloths, and the like. Make sure they are put there when not in use, instead of being tossed into some convenient "glory hole." Use metal containers also for hot ashes and the daily accumulation of papers and trash.

Be certain that electric wiring fuses are in good order. Pennies behind burned-out fuses are a misuse of good money in more ways than one.

Inspect the cords of all electrical appliances and portable lamps. If they are frayed or broken, replace them. Speaking of appliances, the simple flat-iron in the hands of a careless or absent-minded person probably causes more fires than all the other more complicated work-savers combined. For stage-struck Seventeen, then, moodily pressing her pink organdy while mentally sweeping a triumphant course through a crowded ballroom in a sophisticated black model from Paris; or for dark-hued Martha who thumps out on a luckless shirt the damage she plans to inflict on a certain Pullman porter when he shows up at her back door again, provide an iron that cannot over-heat. With a thermostat that turns current on and off, it and the ironing board can remain forgotten for hours. The electric light company may benefit but no fire will result.

Equip fireplaces with screens that fit. If the hearth has begun to disintegrate from many fires, it is time to renew it as well as loose mortar.

Mount stoves or Franklin fireplaces on metal-covered, asbestos-lined bases.

Don't put a rug over the register of the pipeless furnace. It will cause dangerous over-heating and the effect will be disastrous rather than decorative.

Be sure no draperies are near open flames such as candles and portable heaters.

If you have gas or keep any quantity of kerosene or gasoline, don't examine containers by match or candlelight. Use an electric flashlight and turn it on *before* going near such explosives. These dangers may seem obvious but it is astonishing how many times that faulty mechanism known as the genus homo has been guilty of just such follies.

If rubbish is burned on the grounds, use an incinerator. It keeps loose papers from blowing around and starting an incipient blaze in some cherished shrubbery or in the grass itself. I once lost a fine row of small pine trees in such a manner. They would have provided an ample screen from the main highway, had I exercised a little care with my miniature bonfire.

Install portable fire extinguishers. They are inexpensive. One to each floor with an extra one for kitchen and cellar is good fire insurance. Be sure every member of the family knows how to use them. Nearly all fires start in a small way and a shot or two of liquid from one of these machines usually extinguishes any but the most stubborn blaze.

Sometimes, however, outside help is needed. So post the number of the nearest fire department prominently near the telephone. Make sure every one knows where to call, what to say, and how to give clear and distinct road directions.

These are little things. Yet houses have gone up in smoke for want of their application. I know of one instance where a competent but city-bred house man was sent to open a country house for the summer. In the course of the day an oil stove in the kitchen was lighted. The man went to get some drinking water. He returned less than five minutes later to find a corner of the room was in flames. There was no extinguisher at hand and his bucket of water was as nothing. There was a telephone in the house and a fire department equipped with a high-powered chemical machine was less than six miles away. Unhappily the man neither knew of its existence nor how to direct it to the place. By the time he had found help and the department had finally been summoned, it was too late. Neighbors and firemen alike could only look on at a magnificent bonfire, piously lamenting the loss, of course, but getting a vicarious pleasure out of the spectacle.

As an example of foolhardiness on the part of the owner it is perhaps beyond comment. Against it I know of another family that goes to the other extreme. In addition to taking the fire precautions suggested here, they have tacked a small typewritten notice on the back of the front door. It reads:

"STOP

Is the furnace checked

Is the water heater out

Is the range turned off

Is the oil heater upstairs out"

This little evidence of fire-policing has amused many of their guests, but their house is still standing and the fire insurance inspector performs his annual duties in a perfunctory manner after reading it.

Unless there are glaring defects in chimney construction, electric wiring, or furnace flues, these simple details and a reasonable amount of old-fashioned caution will practically keep home fires in their place. For those who wish to cut the fire hazard still further there are more elaborate precautions that involve some rebuilding and renovation. Whether any or all of them are advisable is a matter for the owner and his architect to decide.

If a fireproof cellar is wanted, cover the ceiling with metal lath and a good cement plaster. This should extend up the stairway, and the cellar door should be of fire resisting construction.

Firestopping all exterior walls and interior partitions not only cuts down fire risk but adds greatly to insulation from both heat and cold. Fires that originate in the cellar frequently travel upward in the dead-air spaces behind lath plaster. For houses already built, the best means is to pack the walls with pulverized asbestos. There are contractors who specialize in this work and have equipment for doing the job quickly with minimum cutting and inconvenience.

**AN IMPOSING COUNTRY HOME OF CLASSIC DIGNITY**

*Robertson Ward, architect. Photo by Samuel H. Gottscho*

An electric fire detector in the cellar acts much like a burglar alarm. There are several now on the market. The principle on which they work is thermostatic.

Sensitive to increased heat, an alarm bell sounds the moment fire develops. The White House has one of the most elaborate systems of this sort, which was installed shortly after the executive office fire of a few years ago.

Checking chimneys comes next after leaving the cellar. All chimneys should rest on a solid foundation in the ground. Those carried on wooden beams are never safe. The normal settling will produce dangerous cracks in the joints of the brickwork. Likewise, unused stove-pipe holes should be closed with bricks and mortar cement. Chimneys connected with open fireplaces ought to be equipped with spark arresters. These are simply bronze or brass wire of sufficiently fine mesh to catch any sparks. Placed at the top, they also serve to discourage chimney swallows from nesting in the throat of an old-fashioned chimney, to the doubtful pleasure of the occupants of the house.

For the roof there are slate and non-burnable shingles as well as a system by which weather boarding under wooden shingles can be replaced with panels of fireproof plaster sheathing.

If there is any doubt regarding the condition of electric wiring it will be real economy to have a licensed electrician inspect it and replace any which is obsolete or not in accord with insurance regulations. Also, if steam or hot water pipes go through flooring or are close to the wooden trim, there should be at least three-quarters of an inch clearance. Otherwise, the heat dries and carbonizes the wood. Then slight additional heat may produce spontaneous combustion.

Then there are more elaborate rebuilding projects such as installing a fire sprinkler system in the cellar.

A built-in incinerator located in the cellar with chute opening in the kitchen is excellent for the immediate disposal of trash and rubbish.

Two stairways connecting living and bedroom floors are always better than one. Either stairway should be accessible to any bedroom. An emergency doorway will make this possible.

If the garage is attached to the house it should be lined with a fire resisting material. Metal lath and plaster or a good grade of plaster wall board is preferred. The door between house and garage should, of course, be fire resisting and self closing.

There is one other refinement which the country house owner may take into consideration, especially if he happens to own an historic old house. That is the installation of a system of perforated pipes in the dead air spaces behind all walls connected with storage tanks of carbon dioxide under pressure. If a fire breaks out, turning on this system will flood the house with a gas that will smother all flame. Mount Vernon is a notable example of a house so equipped.

So much for the more or less man-produced fire hazards. There is, however, the occasional fire that comes down from heaven. The National Board of Fire Underwriters has proved by careful investigation that a properly installed and maintained system of lightning rods will give a house ninety-eight per cent protection. It does not prevent the building from being struck, but it does provide an easy and direct path to earth for the lightning discharge, thus preventing damage and destruction. This has nothing to do with the old school of lightning rod sales-men trained in medicine show methods. Proper equipment and competent men working under inspection by the Underwriters Laboratories are now available. Incidentally, radio antennae should be properly grounded and have an approved lightning arrester.

There is one more possibility of disaster from lightning. Ordinary wire fencing mounted on wooden posts can become so highly charged with electricity during a thunder storm that no living thing is safe within thirty feet of it. Proper ground-ing is again the remedy and is relatively simple. At every fifth post an iron stake should be driven deep enough to reach permanent moisture. Connect this to the fencing by a wire tightly wrapped around the stake and each strand of the fencing. This causes the electricity generated during a storm to escape harmlessly into the ground, just as it does through the cables of a properly installed set of lightning rods.

# CHAPTER XVI
## WHEN THINGS GO WRONG

With life in the country, there are times when the innate perverseness of the inanimate asserts itself. For one accustomed to city conditions this is almost a paralyzing experience. There is no apartment house superintendent to call on, no repairman just around the corner. In itself it may be very simple; but what to do, how to do it and with what tools, unless you have gone through the mill, is soul-searing. So, almost as soon as you have established your sources of food and fuel, address yourself to the problem of discovering the neighborhood handy man.

Not all men of the usual mechanical trades can qualify. Such a jewel must have native ingenuity, really enjoy coping with sudden emergencies and, like the old-fashioned country doctor, be possessed of a temperament that accepts sudden calls for help as part of the day's work. He may have planned to take his family to the village moving picture show; but if your plumbing has sprung a leak, your pump has suddenly ceased to function, or any one of a dozen other contingencies has arisen, nothing is so comforting as his assurance that "he'll be right over." You know that within a reasonable time this physician to things mechanical will arrive in his somewhat battered automobile with an assortment of tools and supplies adequate for the majority of minor domestic crises.

Sometimes he can repair the damage permanently then and there. Sometimes his service is of a temporary nature to tide your household over until the proper correction can be accomplished either by him or some other artisan whose specialty it is. At the moment this makes little difference. Several summers ago, our water supply failed most inconsiderately just at dinner time. There was plenty of water in the well and the electric pump was functioning but the storage tank was bone dry. What was wrong was beyond our understanding. Worst of all, our village plumber could not be reached even by a fairly resourceful country telephone central. We called our handy man and were greeted by a cheery if long suffering, "What's the matter *now*?" We told him and most assuringly he replied, "Sounds like foot valve trouble. I'll be right over soon as I finish supper."

And he was as good as his word. Half an hour later he was listening to a pump that could not lure water from well to tank. Then he went down the well and, without aid, came up with the supply pipe. "Here's your trouble. Leather of the foot valve's gone. I'll just cut another." He dived into the rear seat of his car and returned with a square of sole leather. Using the old leather as a pattern he cut a new one with a sharp jack knife and before dark the supply pipe was back in place and the artificial drought was broken. Thanks to the skill and willingness of this all-essential neighborhood personage, there was once more water for dishwashing and family needs.

This is but one instance of how he has come to our rescue and through the years taught us many things that we can now do for ourselves. Although not over-skillful with tools and things mechanical, we have learned that doing them is sometimes the quickest and easiest way out of our difficulties. Some, of course, were beyond the limits of our simple abilities but we hereby enumerate some twenty of the more common difficulties that may arise inopportunely with country living, and what to do about them.

A sudden break in electric service leaves your house dark. The answer to this is a supply of candles and one or two kerosene lamps filled and ready for use, as well as at least one electric flashlight, in working order and hung in its appointed place. Often before the various lamps are assembled and lighted, electricity will again be available; but if service is interrupted for several hours, as occasionally happens with a serious break in the line or real trouble at the power house, you will have cause to bless the auxiliary lighting. Having it to depend on just once will well repay the trouble of making it available. Be sure, also, that you have at least one complete set of extra fuses to repair the damage of a short circuit caused by defective appliances or lamp cords. Never, never put a penny into a fuse socket.

Next to light, the most important creature comfort is water and plenty of it. The most common causes of failure lie with the pump itself. If one of the deep well type gets out of adjustment, repairing it is a professional job and unless you are unusually expert, don't attempt it. Telephone for a plumber or handy man. But with the shallow well pump, you can, in a pinch, replace the leathers that make the valves exert the proper suction. In any case, it is good sense to have an extra set of the leathers always on hand. Near our own pump there is a glass preserving jar half full of neat's-foot oil and, pickling in it, a spare set of pump leathers just waiting for something to happen. We also have a box of assorted faucet washers. It is over a year since we have had to replace one; but when a faucet suddenly refuses to close, we know where the proper valve is located so that we can shut off the water long enough to replace the troublesome washer, usually the work of a few minutes.

Then there is the heating system. Here the most common demonstration of temperament is sulkiness on a heavy damp day. In any event, provided the fire is free from clinkers, we have a standard remedy. An average-sized electric fan is placed before the open ash pit door. Set in motion, its breeze provides a forced draft and, in from fifteen minutes to half an hour, our furnace fire is once more glowing and throwing out heat.

Also, the country house owner, who discovers that furnace or fireplace flues which have heretofore functioned properly are smoking, should investigate the circumstances without delay. The troublesome flue may only need cleaning, or a dislodged brick or other obstacle may have blocked it. Whatever the cause, the chimney should have immediate attention, for excess soot is the common cause of chimney fires. If an excess odor of coal gas indicates that the fumes are filling the cellar instead of going up the chimney, open the hatchway and as many windows as possible. Then check the furnace completely. Investigate the cause of the trouble and you will find that the smoke pipe connecting the furnace and chimney is out of place. Don't try to replace the dislocated pipe until the cellar is thoroughly aired, for furnace fumes can be almost as deadly as those exhausted by an automobile, for the same reason, the presence of carbon monoxide gas. So when working on the pipe be careful to retreat out of doors on the slightest feeling of faintness or other disturbing symptom. The safest way is not to attempt to replace the smoke pipe until the furnace fire is out.

There are one or two other things down cellar that can go awry when least expected. One of the most common is flooding caused by abnormally heavy rains and leaks in foundation walls. Look first for these where the pipes from the eaves, known as down-spouts, reach the ground. Provide dry wells, troughs, or other means to carry this rain water away from the foundation. After your cellar flood has either evaporated or been pumped out and the foundation walls are dry inside and out, repair the cracks through which this water trickled, as well as others that might have contributed to the trouble. Use a rich cement to which has been added the proper amount of water-proofing chemical.

One cannot be over-zealous in this, for a flooded or even damp cellar is always a hazard. Under no circumstances attempt to turn on electric lights if you are standing where it is wet or damp. Ninety-nine times out of a hundred all that can happen is a mild electric shock but there is always the one chance in thousands that by so doing you may be your own electrocutioner. It is safest to have all cellar lights controlled by one or more switches at the head of the cellar stairs; but if there is a light that must be turned on in the cellar itself, leave it alone under conditions of standing water and be sure the fault is rectified before the next heavy rain can cause a repetition.

Just as storms can make trouble below stairs, roof and eaves may develop faults. Where the roof is of wooden shingles, one of the usual causes of leaks is a cracked shingle. When this chances to be directly above a slight space left in laying the roof for expansion between the shingles of the next course, rain, instead of flowing off the roof, runs through this crack and wet plaster results. This does not mean that the roof must be re-laid if otherwise tight and sound. Get a sheet of roofing tin or copper, locate the troublesome crack, and gently insert a piece of the sheet metal, trimmed to the right size, beneath the cracked shingle. Properly done, you should not find it necessary to nail the piece of sheet metal because the shingles themselves will hold it in place. While making this repair, be careful not to walk on the roof more than is absolutely necessary. Your weight and the pressure of your feet may crack other shingles. It is better to work from a ladder. This should have a large iron hook that will catch on the ridgeboard and keep it from slipping. It also distributes the weight of the man making the repair.

Sometimes eaves, instead of providing drainage and conducting rain from the roof to ground, work in the reverse. The dampened plaster of the interior side walls soon betrays this. When these spots appear it is probable that the opening where the down-spout joins the eaves-trough is clogged with leaves and small twigs. Remove this plug that has gradually accumulated round the strainer and once more rain water will flow merrily and noisily down the spout. Also, in winters of unusually heavy snowfalls and cold weather, if the eaves-troughs are hung too close to the edge of the roof or have not sufficient slope for rapid drainage, the snow on the roof melts, drips to the eaves-trough, and freezes before it can flow away. Eventually some of this moisture creeps beneath the shingles and makes ugly damp patches on the plaster beneath. Immediate relief can be had by mounting a ladder, clearing the trough of the ice, and thawing the frozen down-spout with salt and kettles of hot water. Later, the permanent remedy is to have a practical roofer rehang and adjust the eaves-troughs.

Because of the very nature of winter weather, there are other distressing things that may happen to make life in the country just a little bit less enjoyable. The first of these is the possibility of an old-fashioned blizzard that may block roads and cut off the country dweller from the usual source of supplies. Before the days of the automobile, one could travel roads several feet deep in snow with horse and sleigh. An automobile has its limits and is more or less impotent in more than two feet of snow on a road unbroken by a powerful plow. So, if the oldest inhabitants can remember the winter of 18— "when we had snow to the top of the fence posts," it is a wise precaution to have an emergency supply of canned foods on hand. In February, 1934, we were snowbound for three days but lived in comfort, thanks to a minimum reserve supply and, by a happy coincidence, liberal marketing done the morning the storm began. Several neighbors took to snowshoes and skis and so made their way to the nearest store to replenish essentials like milk, meat, eggs and the like. Winter sports are a great institution, but trudging two miles for a quart of milk across a countryside waist deep in newly fallen snow is too great a mixture of business and pleasure.

Similarly, a medicine cabinet stocked with the primary remedies, and a physician whom you know sufficiently so that you consult him by telephone, are wise precautions against sudden crises of weather or health. Of course, if a member of your family is seriously ill, your doctor will come with all haste when summoned. But he is a busy man who often works from before breakfast until nearly midnight covering unbelievable distances in his automobile. So, if you can report illness clearly, give exact symptoms, and have a stock of the simple medicines that you can administer as he directs, both the sick person and the physician gain. Present-day country doctors show their appreciation for such cooperation by the speed with which they reach patients whose symptoms indicate more than a minor ailment.

But all the emergencies of country life are not serious even though they call for action. There are scores of little things that the house owner can do for himself. Take rats and mice. They will get into the most carefully built and best run house. When this happens it is a matter of either traps or the new scientific poison baits that domestic pets will not eat. There is also the old farm method of mixing equal parts of plaster of Paris and corn meal, an entree harmless in itself but with fatal results for the invading rodent. In summer there is the possibility of a plague of ants. For this there is now a cheap and scientific liquid bait that works rapidly.

In summer, also, come those occasional nights of abnormal heat when no breeze stirs. Bedrooms stay hot and sleep is difficult. For this, set an electric fan on the floor of each room, pointed toward the ceiling, with a chair before it to serve as a barricade. The current of air so produced dislodges the hot air in the room that is above the level of the window openings and also provides a mild breeze that does not blow directly on a sleeper. By actual tests with an accurate thermometer, the temperature of a bedroom can be lowered a full five degrees. It is this difference between 80 and 85 degrees that can make an otherwise stifling night bearable enough for refreshing sleep.

Also at the time you want it most, usually with the house full of week-end guests, the hot water supply turns tepid. The means of heating the water is functioning properly but the storage tank is cold. When this happens, unless all water piping is of copper or brass, the chances are better than even that your tank is clogged with rusty sediment. This does not mean a new tank. It is just a matter of draining and flushing until most, if not all, of the sediment is washed out. Turn off the pipe that supplies heater and tank. Then with garden hose attached to the faucet at the base of the tank, drain out all the water that will come. For a thorough job unscrew this faucet and the piece of pipe connecting it to the tank. Then turn on the water supply quickly for two or three minutes at a time so that a sudden flow of clean water disturbs the sediment. At first it may be almost as thick as a heavy soup but gradually the water will become clearer. When it is normal you can replace pipe and faucet, relight the water heater, and forget your hot water supply for at least a year. Of course, it is better to undertake this chore when you are without company, but one must have hot water and, at that, the operation should not take over an hour. Perhaps some of the guests will be big hearted and offer to help.

A plaster ceiling appears to fall without warning. Actually, if you are observant, weak spots can be detected before they reach the falling stage. A slight bulge that gives if you press it upward gently with the fingers is an unfailing indication that the plaster has begun to loosen and that possibly the laths beneath are also loose. The best method of correcting this is, of course, to engage a plasterer. He will remove what is loose and probably much more. Then, having replaced the defective or old lath, he will re-plaster and a properly finished job will result.

There is, however, another course of action. It is neither permanent nor as good but it will bridge a gap when the family exchequer can ill afford the luxury of a plasterer and his helper. This is an old farm method of economical stop-gap repair. Take some new coarse muslin. Make a strong solution of glue sizing; wash the calcimine or whitewash from the ceiling where it is weak; paint with a coat of the size; and when it is almost dry, spread the muslin on like ceiling paper having first dipped it in the size. When the cloth is dry, re-calcimine the ceiling. Such work is not according to the best standards of journeyman work but we have known a ceiling so strengthened to remain in place for some years. This unorthodox trick was taught us by the neighborhood handy man whose praises we sang earlier. Another was the practice of binding a water pipe, that had developed a tiny pin-hole leak, with the black sticky fabric known as friction tape used by electricians. It held for half a year until it was more convenient, financially and otherwise, to have our plumber replace the leaking pipe.

Incidentally, knowing how to thaw a water pipe that has, as countrymen say, "just caught," on some abnormally cold night is also an accomplishment of ingenuity. Too much heat applied too rapidly can crack a pipe. So such work should be done in moderation. Be sure the faucet of the stopped pipe is open. Then, locate the spot by sense of feel. It will be much colder than the rest of the pipe. First try wrapping it in cloths wrung out in hot water. If this does not produce results, gently pour steaming but not boiling water on the pipe from a teakettle. Stop after a minute or two to let the applied heat become effective. If necessary, repeat several times. For stubborn cases, an electric heater directed at the frozen spot can be used effectively.

When hunting for the seat of trouble look at the spot where the pipe comes through the floor. A crack between flooring and baseboard may be the air leak that has caused the trouble. Next examine the pipe along an exterior wall or in the direct range of a window. Frozen pipes concealed in partition walls, unless they are accessible through a panel of removable woodwork, are not for the amateur. They are for a plumber who will know how to reach the trouble without doing other damage.

Many are the expedients that life in the country and friendly chats with your own handy man can teach you. Some of them you will discover for yourself, for necessity, the mother of invention and country living, often presents minor emergencies that the house owner must meet and conquer for himself. That is part of the fun of living in the country. You have escaped the stereotyped city where such things are the concern of apartment house superintendents. In the country it is each man for himself.

# CHAPTER XVII

## WORKING WITH NATURE

In the home owner's dream of country life, green lawns, rose gardens, and shady terraces have loomed large; but in the actual fulfillment, his house has of necessity come first. Beyond a sketchy clearing up of the most obvious debris, he may well come to the end of his first summer with practically nothing done to the grounds themselves. This is not entirely a disadvantage. It has been shown how too much may be done to a house in the first fervor of remodeling or restoration. It is the same with the land surrounding it.

The old adage, "Begin as you can hold out," is an excellent rule to follow. One of the advantages gained by living in an area just beyond the suburban fringe is that one's two, five, or ten acres may be developed as much or as little as one desires or can pay for. This holds whether you have built a new house in the middle of a former pasture or have restored an old one with grounds well developed but long neglected.

Of course, you will not lack for advice from friends and acquaintances, most of the people who have never grown anything more extensive than a window box. They will tell you that the old lawn that has withstood the tread of feet for more than a century is uneven and must be plowed under, re-graded, and a special kind of lawn-grass sown. The driveway is all wrong, too. Turn it back into lawn and build a new one winding through the field to the left where the family cow was once pastured. They are also kind enough to suggest that a plowing, grading, and seeding of this additional acre or so will give you a piece of greensward worth having. A lily pool and sun dial garden would go nicely over there to the east, and how about that hollow place over in the south corner for a swimming pool? All this and much more can be suggested but it is surprising how little of it is practical.

**SKILLFUL PLANTING OF TREES, SHRUBS, AND FLOWERS MAKE THE SETTING**

*Photo by Samuel H. Gottscho. Robertson Ward, architect*

Even long neglected grounds seldom require as thorough a job of face lifting. A lawn free of hollows is difficult to achieve and almost impossible to maintain. Nature does not do things that way, so work with her rather than against her. It is surprising how old and seemingly worn-out grounds respond to kind treatment. Study them first before doing anything. Take stock of existing trees, shrubs and the like. Notice the contour of the land. Then make a simple landscaping plan. This, well thought out, will give direction to the eventual development of the plot of ground you have in mind. Work gradually. If you are reclaiming an old place, remember the original owner did not achieve everything in a week or a year. Nature cannot be hurried. It is true that, if one desires shade trees and cannot wait for them to grow, experts can bring full-grown ones from their nurseries and plant them in the positions you designate. Such practices run into money, however, and would hardly come within the average family budget.

Let us suppose that the home owner finds himself in possession of a house of uncertain age and between ten and twenty acres of land. Unless he is prepared to maintain a miniature conservation corps, he will not attempt to keep over two acres in active cultivation. Even with those he will not push back the wilderness in one season. The first step is a careful inspection of the grounds around the house. If they have been neglected for years, he may find practically anything except grass growing. If the average tenant farmer has lived there any length of time, the area at the back lying at easy tossing distance from the back door may contain a wealth of tin cans, bottles, broken dishes, and other debris. These, of course, must all be picked up and either carried away by the rubbish collector or otherwise disposed of. We have read of clever people who managed to persuade members of their family and any visiting friends that such an undertaking could be made into a sort of treasure hunt and one's grounds cleaned painlessly and without added expense. It did not work with our family. A cache of twenty-five fine rusty cans nestling under the lilacs elicited nothing beyond a mild query as to the likelihood of lily of the valley thriving in the spot.

So we hired the man whose family had spent ten long years accumulating the debris, to clean the half acre surrounding the house and he made a very neat workmanlike job of it. Afterward he commented on the improved appearance, especially of the back yard. "Yes, it looks considerable better," he said, "but of course I couldn't keep it that way. I'm a poor man and my time is worth sixty cents an hour. I can't afford to spend any of it picking up after myself."

His philosophy is apparently not uncommon and one may expect to find anything on the land from rusty scythe blades to broken down farm wagons and automobiles. After these have been removed the place will look decidedly improved even though a mossy growth under the maples denotes sour soil, and burdocks and milkweed in the back indicate good soil gone wrong. Along with ridding the grounds of rubbish comes the question of what to do with the various outbuildings. Those that can be put to practical use should be repaired and their foundations pointed up. Any others should be torn down as a dilapidated structure of any sort is not only unsightly but a breeding place for rats.

As this ordinary cleaning and furbishing progresses, the new owner begins to get really acquainted with his place and discover what exists in the line of shrubs, trees, and vines. There may even be a few flowers that have survived years of neglect. If he is wise, he will prune and preserve all these as a nucleus. Around them he can build his general landscaping plan.

Preserve old trees wherever possible. Even those that appear so stricken by age and neglect as to be ready for firewood often take on a new lease of life after a good tree surgeon has ministered to them. A long neglected lawn, or even a field that has been allowed to run to tall grass, can be reclaimed quite simply. Go over it early in the spring with a heavy roller to get rid of minor hollows and general unevenness. Thin, worn spots, where it is obvious that no grass has grown for years, should be fortified with a load or two of good top soil, rolled and planted to grass seed. Other spots, usually under shade trees where there is the mossy growth of sour soil, should be sprinkled liberally with lime. Repeated treatments will soon correct this condition and grass can again be made to grow there. As soon as the grass is of proper length begin to cut it with the lawn mower. Also, continued applications of the weighted iron roller throughout the spring will gradually improve the general contour and make for smoothness and ease in lawn mowing.

This is strenuous work both for the lawn mower and the person operating it. The former will probably be nearly worn out by the end of the summer, so in choosing this tool get a good but not too elaborate one. Later, when the grounds are in good condition will be time enough to indulge in the better grades of hand or even power driven lawn mowers. Likewise, we do not recommend the task of either rolling or breaking in a lawn to a man who has led a sedentary life for years. It will be cheaper in the long run to engage a muscular individual in the locality who understands and is accustomed to such work. Whether such an one is engaged by the hour, day, week or year, we would add a word of warning based on our own blundering experiences. Beyond being sober, honest, and willing, make sure he is strong enough for such heavy work, that he is reasonably intelligent and, most important of all, that he is not "working to accommodate." The latter is frequently voiced by members of decadent native families who resent the curse of Adam and like to assume that any gesture toward the hated thing, called work, is purely voluntary rather than necessary. If these words fall from the lips of a man you are considering for odd jobs and tilling of the soil, leave him severely alone and look for a good energetic individual who knows he was made to work and is glad of it. Otherwise, the "accommodating" one will condescendingly show up for work an hour late, regard you with a pitying smile as you outline the job, and then allow that of course you are the boss but you are going at it all wrong. When, after lengthy discussion of how an intelligent country-born person would arrange matters, he senses that the evil moment of going to work can no longer be put off, he directs his lagging steps to the spot where the tools are waiting. These he regards with blackest pessimism. His attitude is that only a city moron would provide such poor things but, of course, he will do the best he can with them. In the course of the day he gets a little work done but in such sketchy fashion that most of it must be done over.

Nor does he improve as the days go by. When you decide to part with him, probably soon after your first inspection of his work, you will get a fresh shock at the size of his bill. Such people have an exaggerated idea of the value of their services. It is difficult to get them to name a price at the beginning; and in the rare cases where a set sum is agreed upon, the final reckoning will invariably include certain extras or a plaint that "the job was different than you claimed and I don't do heavy work like that for nobody without I get extra pay and I was just working to accommodate—" and so forth. Usually you end by paying him and charging it off to experience.

This does not mean that there is no good local labor. It is just a matter of determining which man is actually "a good worker" and which would rather lean on a hoe and tell how the country ought to be run. You can avoid much labor turnover and unsatisfactory work if you first ask a few questions of substantial members of the countryside who are in the habit of employing such men and therefore know their good and bad points. One man may be strong and willing but so stupid and clumsy that he destroys more than he earns; another may be deft, ingenious, have an uncanny way with flowers and vegetables, but yet have such an utter lack of responsibility that one cannot depend on him for any length of time.

Assuming then that a good, dependable man has been found who understands and has a liking for the soil, the task of helping nature to bring out the best in your grounds progresses to those parts afflicted by such rank weeds as burdocks, thistles, milkweed, poison ivy and the like. Weeds with the long tap root like burdock and yellow dock can be eliminated best with a mattock. With one sharp blow, cut the root two or three inches below the surface. Then pull up the top and toss it aside where it will wither in the sun. What is left in the ground also dies and will not sprout. A Canadian thistle is really a handsome sight especially in full bloom but it is a thoroughly unpleasant weed and must be eradicated. Dig up each plant with a spading fork or sharp shovel and leave it to wither in the July sun, its roots shaken free of earth. Milkweed is persistent but will finally yield if the stalks are consistently pulled up as soon as they are three or four inches tall.

For poison ivy there is one preliminary. Be sure you are not one of the people readily susceptible to its poison. If you are, leave this luxuriant parasite alone and let some one else struggle with it. Its poison is most virulent in the spring when the leaves are just unfolding. Later in the summer it is not so treacherous. Tearing it up by the roots, burning over old stone fences infected with it, keep it from overrunning a place; but the most satisfactory method of eradicating is to sprinkle the vines with sodium arsenite. This, by tests at various agricultural stations, has lately been found a sure means of killing this most unpleasant of all vegetable pests that infect the countryside.

Along with getting a reasonable expanse of green grass, the simple landscaping plan already referred to should be kept in mind. If you have but a vague idea concerning this and, as time goes on, tend to become more confused and undecided as to what kind of flowers, shrubs, and vines would be most suitable or how they should be arranged, consult the best nurseryman in your vicinity, if he has not already visited you. All of the larger nurseries now have on their staffs experienced landscape architects. Many of them are recent graduates of the recognized schools in this field and, for the asking, you can have a simple landscape plan for your grounds. Such nurseries do this, of course, in expectation that if the plan is accepted the needed small trees, shrubs, and hardy perennials will be bought of them.

In fact, when the plan is submitted, it will probably be accompanied by a tentative list of the needed plants. These you can buy either delivered ready for planting, or a somewhat higher price will include this service by men from the nursery. In the latter case, the nursery usually guarantees that everything supplied will live for a year or be replaced without charge. Personally, we have found that the nearer home we bought nursery stock, the better were its chances of living and thriving. There is no adjustment to different climatic conditions and such plants and shrubs are only a very short time out of the soil before they are planted in your grounds either by you or the man sent from the nursery. Nearly always they put their roots down and continue growing with little or no interruption.

The matters of gardens, flower beds, and borders again depend on the contour of the land and how it can best be related to the house. Further, unless you are well versed in gardening, it is best to get advice as to the flowers and plants that thrive best in a given spot. It is discouraging to lay out a rose garden or a modest border of hardy climbers and find you have picked just the wrong place for them to thrive. It is the same with certain perennials.

Rock gardens are most picturesque and lend themselves to a large variety of hardy and interesting plants. The most successful are those where nature supplies the framework. One of the loveliest we ever saw had originally been a pigsty. Halfway up a hillside two large boulders jutted out and below them a rocky formation descended in shelf-like steps to a level surface. Ingenious planting and patient care transformed this into a mass of color and bloom that has been admired for miles. Its owner has gradually expanded it and has even added rocks dug from a neighboring field. The farmer who supplied them shook his head resignedly. "Well, I've lived in these parts a long time and seen plenty of queer things. I can understand paying a man to dig out rocks but this is the first time I was ever asked to dump them on good land."

The formal garden is usually part of the development of the very ambitious country estate. Such grounds are the result of plans prepared by a practicing landscape architect, engaged on a fee basis as with other architects. According to the arrangements he will prepare the plans or he will also supervise their execution. While there are some remarkable formal gardens in America, beautifully designed and kept in perfect condition by skillful gardeners engaged by the year, most homes do not have such sophisticated settings.

Popular indeed is an area of well-kept lawn surrounded by naturalistic plantings of trees, shrubs, and hedges that give privacy and frame the whole. Add to this borders of flowering plants, annuals and perennials, and from spring to late fall such a spot becomes an outdoor living room. Here the family spends most of its time. Real enthusiasts eat many of their meals here.

As for the vegetable garden, keep it small. The new country dweller's first garden is usually three times the size needed or that he can take care of. Vegetables have a way of either producing nothing or bearing in such abundance that the average family is swamped in plenty. Whether or not the excess is canned, depends on the time and energy of the housewife or her cook. With green vegetables now available the year around, there are two schools of thought as to the real economy of home canning. There is even plenty of controversy over the question of a family vegetable garden. Some hold that after the normal charges for fertilizer, seeds and labor are met, any vegetables that may result actually cost far more than if bought in the retail market. To this the pro-gardenites retort that the charges for seeds and fertilizer are small and that a certain amount of struggle with spade and hoe is good for a man who has spent all day in a stuffy office. Let him do his own spading, cultivating, and planting. A half hour or so every evening will keep the garden free of weeds and, in due time, vegetables fresh from the garden will result. They will be superior in flavor and will actually have cost less than even the largest chain stores can afford to sell them for.

Out of ten years' experience, we can only state that both are right in a measure. Whether or not a vegetable garden pays, breaks even, or goes into the red, depends to a large degree on the owner himself. If he has a flair for making things grow and has a definite amount of time to devote to them, his garden will not only thrive but pay dividends. But if a business trip is imperative just at the time the garden should be planted, or some pressing engagement causes him to defer transplanting his cabbages and his tomato plants beyond the proper time, he must either get some one to take care of his garden or do without one. There is a lure, however, to having your own vegetables, so most of us close our eyes to any distressing figures on the household ledger and go ahead and have a garden anyway.

One busy man compromises by having his garden prepared for planting by a local man of all work who also keeps his grass cut and his borders trimmed. Then he plants a few easily grown and tended vegetables, such as lettuce, parsley, string beans, carrots, spinach, crookneck squash, tomatoes, and corn. Around these, like a border, he plants showy annuals like zinnias, cosmos, calendula, marigolds and so forth. His garden is a colorful, attractive spot. He has vegetables for the table and plenty of flowers for cutting. The latter preclude any argument over whether his garden pays since, oddly enough, the subject of a flower garden never seems to take a mercenary turn.

Distinct additions to the kitchen garden are an herb bed, a few rhubarb plants, and an asparagus bed. The latter, because it takes time to become established, seems difficult but laying out a proper bed is not so hard. Also, in two to three years the plants will have reached the stage where the larger stalks may be cut for consumption. At first this should be done judiciously in order not to kill the plants but after another year or two the bed will yield consistently. After it is well established, it provides the first home-grown vegetables of spring and bears for about six weeks. Afterwards all it requires is an occasional weeding and fall mulching with fertilizer and leaves.

As for the tools that keep gardens and grounds in condition, a special shed is advisable. Don't try to keep them in a tool house or section given over to saws, planes, chisels and bits. They get in a hopeless jumble. Nothing is more discouraging than to go out to what should be a tidy little spot to do a bit of mending or minor job of carpentry and find earth encrusted garden trowels, weeders, and such gear scattered all over the work bench. The grit so adhering is fatal to sharp-edged tools, while sprays, dusting powders, and fertilizers give off fumes that rust them.

We would also add a few kind words for the various berries and small fruits. Except for strawberries, which must be kept weeded and replanted periodically, berries are our ideal of easily cared for fruits. Raspberries, for instance, never become really cheap in the market because of their perishable nature. Yet with the very minimum of care, cutting out old canes after the bearing season is over and keeping weeds down with a mulch of hay, a comparatively small patch of red raspberries, within three years of planting, will produce all the fruit an average family can eat or be willing to pick. The other variety, known as "black caps," are no more trouble and equally prolific. These are at their best in pie and, for the pleasures of a succession of fresh black raspberry pies each summer, we heartily recommend planting a dozen canes at the same time that the red raspberry patch is started.

Blackberry canes grow so rankly and bear such brutal thorns that the annual crop seems hardly worth the torn clothing and bad scratches that gathering them entails, especially as they are to be had at such reasonable prices in the average market. Blueberries are another matter. Three or four good bushes of the kind offered by most nurseries will keep the family in blueberry pie with little effort on the part of the person who gathers them. Currants and gooseberries are easily grown but have one serious fault. These bushes harbor plant pests that work havoc with evergreens and a number of the ornamental shrubs. For that reason we long ago eradicated any growing on our place.

Then there are the various fruit trees, cherry, peach, pear, and apple. All of these, for a successful yield, require consistent care and pruning. They must be sprayed at certain seasons for scale and pest or the crop will be meager and poor. With dwarf trees now grown by all nurseries, proper care can be given with simple equipment and there is no doubt that home-grown fruits that are tree-ripened are sweeter and of fuller flavor than those that come from the market. So a few of these trees may well be an addition to your country place, but plant them knowing the care required.

A grape arbor is a most attractive feature and since pruning can be done any pleasant winter day, the work of tending a few vines is so small as to be hardly worth considering. In September it is a real pleasure to stray past the arbor and pluck a bunch of Niagara, Catawba, or Concord grapes and eat them on the spot. So for decoration and fruit borne, a few grape vines are more than worth the slight attention they require.

By working thus intelligently with Nature, you will enjoy her bounties—and this, after all, is the supreme reward offered by a country home.

Lector House believes that a society develops through a two-fold approach of continuous learning and adaptation, which is derived from the study of classic literary works spread across the historic timeline of literature records. Therefore, we aim at reviving, repairing and redeveloping all those inaccessible or damaged but historically as well as culturally important literature across subjects so that the future generations may have an opportunity to study and learn from past works to embark upon a journey of creating a better future.

This book is a result of an effort made by Lector House towards making a contribution to the preservation and repair of original ancient works which might hold historical significance to the approach of continuous learning across subjects.

HAPPY READING & LEARNING!

LECTOR HOUSE LLP
E-MAIL: lectorpublishing@gmail.com

www.ingramcontent.com/pod-product-compliance
Lightning Source LLC
LaVergne TN
LVHW091147180726
843490LV00004B/1345